Sounds Easy!

Phonics, Spelling, and Pronunciation

Photocopiable Exercises for Grades Five to Adult

Sharron Bassano

with Jamie Cross

Illustrations by Karyn Panganiban

Acquisitions Editor: Aaron Berman
Content Editor: Jamie Cross
Cover and Interior Art: Karyn Panganiban
Interior Design: Solomon's Design Studio
Cover Design: Leigh McLellan

The author extends deepest gratitude to Jamie Cross for her creative suggestions for the improvement of this book and for tenacious, skillful editing and proof-reading over and above the call of duty.

ALTA BOOK CENTER PUBLISHERS
14 Adrian Court
Burlingame, California 94010 USA
Phone: 800 ALTA/ESL · 650.692.1285—Int'l
Fax: 800 ALTA/FAX · 650.692.4654—Int'l
Email: info@altaesl.com · Website: www.altaesl.com

ISBN: 1-882483-86-3
ISBN: 978-1-882483-86-0
Library of Congress Control Number: 2001095444

CONTENTS

For Whom is This Book Intended? vii

Teacher's Guide 1

Dictation and Answer Key 9

Section One: Consonants *(Photocopiable Exercises)* 45

b c d f 46
g l m p 47
Review b c d f g l m p 48
t h s k 49
Review b c d f g l m p t h s k 50
r j n v plus Review 51
q w x z plus Review 52
Review 53
Review 54
y—Two Sounds 55
g—Two Sounds 56
c—Two Sounds 57
p and b Contrast 58
d and t Contrast 59
g and ck Contrast 60
l and r Contrast 61
h and j Contrast 62
v and w Contrast 63
b and v Contrast 64
sh and ch Contrast 65
ph and th 66
Review 67
Review 68
Review 69
Review 70

Section Two: Vowels (Photocopiable Exercises) 71

LETTER	SOUND		
a	can	Picture Page	72
a	can	Read/Write	73
a	cake	Picture Page	74
a	cake	Spelling patterns for a	75
a	can/cake	Compare two sounds of a	76
i	gift	Picture Page	77
i	gift	Read/Write	78
i	fire	Picture Page	79
i	fire	Spelling patterns for i	80

i	gift/fire	Compare two sounds of i	81
e	bell	Picture Page	82
e	bell	Read/Write	83
e	tree	Picture Page	84
e	tree	Spelling patterns for e	85
e	bell/tree	Compare two sounds of e	86
o	clock	Picture Page	87
o	clock	Read/Write	88
o	boat	Picture Page	89
o	boat	Spelling patterns for o	90
o	clock/boat	Compare two sounds of o	91
u	truck	Picture Page	92
u	truck	Read/Write	93
u	tube	Picture Page	94
u	tube	Spelling patterns for u	95
u	truck/tube	Compare two sounds of u	96
a	talk	Picture Page	97
a	talk	Spelling patterns for a	98
a	can/talk	Compare two sounds of a	99
a		Review sounds of a	100
i/a	fire/cake	Compare two sounds	101
i/a		Compare four sounds	102
a/o	can/clock	Compare two sounds	103
a/o	can/clock	Compare two sounds	104
i/e	gift/tree	Compare two sounds	105
i/e	gift/tree	Compare two sounds	106
a/e	can/bell	Compare two sounds	107
a/e	can/bell	Compare two sounds	108
a/u	can/truck	Compare two sounds	109
a/u	can/truck	Compare two sounds	110
u/o	truck/clock	Compare two sounds	111
u/o	truck/clock	Compare two sounds	112
Review		. . . .	113
Review		. . . .	114
Review		. . . .	115
Review		. . . .	116
Review		. . . .	117

Section Three: Initial Clusters (Photocopiable Exercises) 119

(bl) 120

(br) 121

(bl)—(br) Compare 122

(pl) 123

(pr) 124

(pl)—(pr) Compare 125

Review Vocabulary (bl)—(br)—(pl)—(pr) 126
(cl) 127
(cr) 128
(cl)—(cr) Compare 129
(gl) 130
(gr) 131
(gl)—(gr) Compare 132
Review Vocabulary (cl)—(cr)—(gl)—(gr) 133
Review Vocabulary (bl)—(br)—(pl)—(pr)—(cl)—(cr)—(gl)—(gr) 134
(fl) 135
(fr) 136
(fl)—(fr) Compare 137
(tr) 138
(dr) 139
(tr)—(dr) Compare 140
Review Vocabulary (fl)—(fr)—(tr)—(dr) 141
(th)—(thr) 142
Review Vocabulary 143
Review Vocabulary (fl)—(fr)—(tr)—(dr)—(th)—(thr) 144
(sp)—(spr)—(spl) 145
(st)—(str) 146
(sm)—(sn)—(sl) 147
Review Vocabulary (s + consonant) 148
Review Vocabulary (s + consonant) 149
(sc)—(scr)—(sq)—(sk) 150
Review Vocabulary (s + consonant) 151
(sh)—(shr) 152
Review Vocabulary 153
Review Vocabulary 154
Review Vocabulary 155
Review Vocabulary 156
Review Vocabulary 157

Section Four: Final Clusters (Photocopiable Exercises) 159

Final b clusters 160
Final p clusters 161
Compare final b and p clusters 162
Final d and t clusters 163
Compare final b, p, d, and t clusters 164
Final ch clusters 165
Final g clusters 166
Final sh clusters 167
Compare final ch, g, and sh clusters 168
Review Vocabulary 169
Final g clusters 170

Final k clusters 171
Final x clusters 172
Compare final g, k, and x clusters 173
Final f and v clusters 174
Final f and v clusters 175
Final ld and lt clusters 176
Final r clusters 177
Final l clusters 178
Compare final r and l clusters 179
Review Vocabulary 180
Final rt and rd clusters 181
Final rl clusters 182
Final rf and rv clusters 183
Review Vocabulary 184
Final rn and rm clusters 185
Final g and ch clusters 186
Final rb and rp clusters 187
Final rs clusters 188
Final rk clusters 189
Review Vocabulary 190
Review Vocabulary 191
Review Vocabulary 192
Review Vocabulary 193
Final nt and nd clusters 194
Final n clusters 195
Final m clusters 196
Final mp clusters 197
Final nch and nge clusters 198
Final ng and nk clusters 199
Review Vocabulary 200
Review Vocabulary 201
Review Vocabulary 202
Final sk and sc clusters 203
Final st clusters 204
Final z and s clusters 205
Review Vocabulary 206
Final th clusters 207

Reference Charts (Photocopiable) . . . . **.209**

Alphabet Chart 210
Consonants Chart 211
Vowels Chart 212
Initial Clusters Chart 213
Final Clusters Chart 214

FOR WHOM IS THIS BOOK INTENDED?

This resource book was created especially for beginning English language learners who have minimal academic background—those who are often mystified by texts, exercise books, written explanations, printed instructions, and worksheets in their new language.

It is intended for students who are learning the English alphabet and its sound system concurrent with building active vocabulary, listening, and oral communication skills. The student may or may not be pre-literate in his or her native language.

The exercises are appropriate for grades five through adult education and are meant to supplement and enhance the core listening and speaking textbook.

The aim is to introduce:

- 21 consonants and their most common pronunciations,

- 5 vowels and the different sounds they produce when standing alone or in combinations,

- 26 of the most common consonant clusters occurring in English in the initial position, and

- 98 of the most common consonant clusters occurring in English in the final position.

On the photocopiable pages you will find no charts, explanations, or diagrams. Neither are there detailed instructions, complex spelling rules, fine print, or extraneous words. Please refer to the Teacher's Guide, page 1 for guidance. We have included only the basic pictures and key words on the student pages for two reasons:

1. Only you, the teacher, know how much explanation your students will comprehend—you know their background, their strengths, needs, previous schooling, and goals. Except for the brief teacher's guide that gives suggestions for sequencing and tasks, we leave instruction in the hands of the expert—you.

2. As your students may not be able to decode written instructions, explanations, or rules, the format and sequence of *Sounds Easy!* allows spelling rules to be deduced. The clean, plain, uncluttered pages help learners center their attention and discover commonalities and patterns. We want to eliminate the confusion and anxiety often experienced by pre- or semi-literate learners when they face text in their new language.

The exercises in *Sounds Easy!* bring feelings of immediate success, accomplishment, and confidence through easy-to-follow, predictable pages. They also encourage study well beyond the introductory experience.

Teacher's Guide

SECTION ONE: CONSONANTS

Twenty-one consonants and their most common sounds

GENERAL SUGGESTIONS

1. Before using the exercises in this book, hand out a stack of 3 x 5 cards to each student. Have students create their own personal set of alphabet cards with marker pens. Give them each an envelope to keep the cards in for their notebooks or binders. Do a variety of activities with these cards during each lesson. For example:

   a. Write a letter on the board. Name it. Students find the same letter on their cards and hold it up to show you.

   b. Call out previously studied letters. Students find the right cards and hold them up.

   c. Call out words that begin with letters students have previously studied. Have students hold up the card with the letter.

   d. Call out previously studied letters that spell short words. Students find the letters on their cards, arrange them on their desks, and read them. Leave out the vowels—just have students line up the consonants.

   e. Call out short words. Students find any letters that they think are in those words and arrange them on their desks.

   f. Show a picture (on an overhead projector or in a magazine). Students tell you (as a group) what it is and hold up what they think is the initial sound.

2. Begin each lesson with the *Consonants Chart* on page 211 (you can photocopy this chart for each student, or make transparencies and show it on the overhead projector, or make a wall chart to keep up in the room). Place the new lesson in its larger context and focus students' attention. For example: For the lesson on page 49, "t-h-s-k," review the names and sounds of the consonants previously studied "b-c-d-f g-l-m-p," having students give examples of words that start with those letters. Write the words on the board. Then preview the letters presented in the new lesson, giving examples of words students already know that begin with those letters.

3. To give your students instant feedback on their work, write the correct answer on the board or overhead a few seconds after each letter is dictated—before going on to the next one. Remember we are teaching, not testing. Let students see how they are doing as they are doing it and make their own corrections. As they gain more confidence and skill, you can save the feedback for the end of the lesson.

4. We assume that many of the pictures will be easily identified orally by at least some of your learners. Sometimes the meaning of the illustration will not be immediately clear—either to you or your students. We suggest that you use this occurrence to promote conversation among the students as you all try to clarify the meaning of the picture. Remember that guesswork or speculation is a talent and comfort we are trying to cultivate in our learners to help them cope with ambiguous input often encountered in the creative process of learning a second language. All answers and intentions are given in the answer key, however!

PAGES 46 THROUGH 52

1. After introducing the names and sounds of the letters to be studied for the day (as on the previous page), write them in random order on the board and say their names. For example:
Say: The name of the letter is . . .
b c d f b b c d d d b f b c f d d f f f b d

Practice the letters aloud with the whole class. Ask volunteers to try it.

2. Practice the sounds that the letters make. (It will, of course, be necessary to tack on a vowel with each consonant in order to pronounce it. We feel that the /u/ as in *but* is possibly the most practical, as it is the most used vowel sound in our language.)
Say: The sound of the letter is . . .
/buh/ /kuh/ /duh/ /fuh/ /buh/ /buh/ /kuh/

Practice the letter sounds aloud with the class. Ask for volunteers to try it.

Note: Do not write the above transcription of sounds on the board.

3. Do the same as above, saying the letter names at random, and have students write the letters on the first set of lines on the page. Then dictate again, this time the sounds and ask students to write the corresponding letter on the second set of lines.

4. Dictate the names of the pictures one at a time. If possible, ask students to tell you what they see or know. More often than not students can name most of the pictures orally. Ask them to guess at the correct consonants to fill in. Some students will need more modeling from you, others figure it out immediately. Students can copy each other or wait for your feedback if necessary. When all pictures are labeled, read them again in chorus or as single volunteers.

5. The next section is more abstract and therefore a little harder, as there are no pictures to signal meaning. Tell students, "The meaning is not important for right now. Just listen carefully and write the letters you hear." In this brief context, as an exercise in listening and transcribing, the ambiguity is okay. Some groups will not respond to this ambiguity; others will like it as a letter "guessing game." Get them started and see how they do. Most of the words presented are common vocabulary that will come up in books 1 or 2 of your core text series. Other words may be more obscure but are given as practice.

PAGES 53 THROUGH 54

These review pages are conducted as previously outlined and contain only previously practiced letters. After the pictures have been labeled, read them together as a group. Then you might try a sort of "lotto." Call out labels at random. Students find the picture/word that you call and make an "X" on it. Those that scan quickly will look for the word; others may look for the picture. Still others will copy what their partners are doing. There are a lot of ways to learn!

PAGES 55, 56, AND 57

These pages introduce letters that have two distinct sounds, determined by their position in a word or by their combination with different vowels. Conduct the exercises as described on the previous page.

PAGES 58 THROUGH 65

1. These pages feature "minimal pairs"—sounds and letters that are often confused for their similarities, both in writing and in speaking. Each picture and each dictation will require only those two letters (for example, only *r* or *l* or only *h* or *j*). No other letters are needed. Conduct these pages as previously described, including crossing out or circling words that you call out at random after students have labeled the pictures.

2. As another alternative for practicing these minimal pairs, you might try working with "interaction grids." Each student is given a piece of 9 x 12 construction paper on which to make a numbered grid (see below). Have them cut out the labeled pictures so that they each have a set of ten cards. Call out these cards at random so students can place them on their grid. For example:

Teacher says:

Number 1—boat. Number 2—vest.
Number 3—vote. Number 4—van.
Number 5—best, etc.

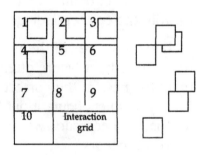

Students place the appropriate card on the numbered grid space. If they do well, have them work with a partner, giving each other instructions as to where to place the picture cards on the grid.

Hint: Make sure students scribble out the tiny number printed on each picture so that they do not confuse this number with the large one on the grid!

PAGE 66

This page briefly points out two combinations—*ph* and *th*. It makes students aware that four of the letters they have learned previously produce entirely different sounds when combined. The combinations are given on the same page not because of similarity, but rather because of their variability. Students will need a lot more practice with *th* and *ph* before the pronunciation and spelling is mastered!

PAGES 67 THROUGH 70

These review pages include all previously practiced letters and sounds and are conducted as described previously for pages 53 and 54.

SECTION TWO: VOWELS

Focusing on five vowels and a variety of sounds they produce when standing alone or in combinations.

GENERAL SUGGESTIONS

Begin each lesson by referring your learners to the *Vowels Chart* on page 212 (you can photocopy this chart for each student, or make transparencies and show it on the overhead projector, or make a wall chart to keep up in the room). This preview is meant to place the new lesson in its larger context and focus students' attention.

PICTURE PAGE

Each of the eleven vowel sounds in this section is introduced with a picture page to allow students to offer something they already know to the class. Let your group brainstorm the labels for each picture, asking, "Who knows the name of one of the pictures?" or, "Who can tell us what number 7 is?" As the students volunteer what they know or guess, write the words on the board or overhead and ask students to copy the words under the pictures.

After the pictures have been labeled, read them through all together. Ask a couple of volunteers to try it. Play a modified "lotto" by calling out one of the words and having students "X" it out. Or allow students to take turns calling the words out for the class to cross off. Those that scan quickly will look for the word; others may look for the picture. Still others will copy what their partners are doing. There are a lot of ways to learn!

READ

After relating a specific and isolated vowel sound to a visual image, students are given the opportunity to read a list of words containing that sound as a practice and confidence builder and to help students extrapolate or infer rule consistency. The "Read" section is more abstract and therefore a little harder; there are no pictures to signal meaning. Tell students, "The meaning is not important for right now. Just experiment with the letters and sounds." Have students read along with you in chorus or in small groups. A couple of volunteers could try it for the class or they may pair up and take turns reading the lists with a partner. Most of the words presented are common vocabulary that will come up in books 1 or 2 of your core text series. Other words may be more obscure but are given as practice.

WRITE

As the third step, dictate twelve of the words from the "Read" list in random order. According to the level of proficiency in your classroom, students may:

- scan the list and underline the words that you say, or
- scan the list and write the words you say on the lines provided, or

- cover the list and write the words you say on the lines provided from memory or by sounding them out.

Note: In this brief context, exercises in decoding, listening, scanning and transcribing—even when the meaning of all the words is not apparent—is pedagogically sound. However, be aware that though some students will respond well—likening it to a letter "guessing game"—others may resist the ambiguity. Just try it. Get them started and see how they do. Then decide on its value.

TROUBLEMAKERS

Troublemakers are words that don't follow the apparent spelling "rules." These are high-frequency words that students must learn to spell and pronounce by rote memorization. Practice them a few times as a group. Use them in oral sentences. Perhaps have students transcribe them into the phonics or alphabet of their primary language. For example, a Spanish speaker might make the notation for "says" as "ses," for "hi" as "jai."

COMPARE

The "Compare" sections are made up mostly of minimal pair words, placed randomly, from which your students will choose and write from your dictation. This gives them the opportunity to use discriminatory skills gained in the preliminary picture exercise and to draw on any spelling or pronunciation rule they have become aware of. The initial "Compare" sections include a contrast of the long and short pronunciation of one vowel, for example, *a* and *a* or *i* and *i*. Other pages present practice with contrasting commonly confused minimal pairs such as *a* and *o* or *i* and *e* and offer extra visual referents.

REVIEW

Five pages of review are included to offer a greater challenge and to assess learning. These sections contain a mixture of all eleven vowel sounds (including many minimal pairs) to choose from in the dictation and reading. Upon completion of this section, it will be apparent who still needs more assistance in recognizing and distinguishing sounds and spelling patterns.

SENTENCE PRACTICE

Several sections have been included that offer short, controlled sentences for reading practice. These sentences focus on the vowel sounds being practiced in that particular lesson and should be easy to decode. For students with basic listening comprehension and verbal skills but lower reading and writing proficiency, these short sentences are an extra reinforcement of their learning. If your students are not yet at a level to derive meaning from these sentences, you may be able to make the meanings clear through actions, objects, and/or pictures. If not, by all means, skip over this section.

SECTION THREE AND FOUR: CLUSTERS

Twenty-six of the most common initial consonant clusters and ninety-eight final consonant clusters.

Begin each lesson by referring your learners to either the *Initial Clusters Chart* on page 213 or the *Final Clusters Chart* on page 214 in this book. You can photocopy these charts for each student, make transparencies and show them on an overhead projector, or make a wall chart to keep up in the room. This preview is meant to place the new lesson in its larger context and focus students' attention.

NAME IT!

Wherever pictures are presented, allow students, as a group, to guess at the vocabulary depicted and at the correct spelling. Use this "brainstorm" time to stimulate conversation. Ask them, "Which ones do we already know?" "Who can tell us what number 8 is?" "Does anyone have any ideas about number 214?" "Yes, I think that is right . . . How should we spell that one?" etc. As the correct answers are arrived at, write them on the board for all the students to copy on their pages. We suggest that as you are writing each word on the board, you give it as much expansion as possible, reminding your students of the contexts in which that item is found. For example, "Yes . . . that *is* a bru*sh*." "What kind of bru*sh* is it?" "A toothbru*sh* . . . shoe bru*sh* . . . oh . . . maybe it's a hair bru*sh*." "Do you think it is for bru*sh*ing a dog? I don't know." "Oh, I see . . . it's for fixing your hair. In the bathroom. Maybe it's on the sink." etc.

When all the pictures on a page have been labeled, you might then dictate definitions or sentences to the class as clues and have them tell you which picture you are referring to. For example: "I'm going to work. I'd better fix my hair . . ." ("Bru*sh*!") "Boy, is this kitchen floor dirty!" ("Wa*sh*!"). If your class is verbal enough, perhaps they could give the clues or definitions for each other. Have them make up the context and answer in pairs, or even have them do the defining and contextualization and you guess the word.

READ • ADD

After your students have had the opportunity to relate a particular spelling configuration (cluster) to a visual image for meaning, they are given a chance to read a list of words containing that cluster as a reinforcement of the spelling pattern and to allow for pronunciation practice. Some of the words they will know the meanings of—others they may not. Tell them that for the moment, meaning is not important. Suggest that they look carefully at the spelling and practice the sound. Have them read along with you in chorus or in small groups for anonymity in practice. Someone may want to try reading the list solo for the class. Also, you might want to pair the students up, asking one to read the list in random order while his or her partner points to the words he or she reads. We personally feel no hesitation in assigning brief practice sessions of no-sense words (where the meaning is unknown) for the specific purpose of reading and reinforcing a spelling/pronunciation pattern. After reading down the "Read" list, have the students write in the missing letters—one at a time, pausing to pronounce the change with each word pair. "Rake" (write in *b*), "brake;" "rag" (write in *b*), "brag," etc. This practice should be brisk! Obviously, where the difference in meaning is not immediately clear, motivation to distinguish and produce the separate sounds is diminished. Keep it short and lively; move about the room during this practice to be sure that everyone is following along.

LISTEN • READ • WRITE

These sections may be handled in the following two ways, depending on your students' proficiency level.

- Ask the students to listen to the sentence as you read it and you supply the missing word. They will locate the missing word that you have supplied in either the picture section or in the reading list and write it in the space provided. After completing the sentences, have students check their pages with a partner to see if they have both understood and written the same word. Then you might write the correct words on the board for a final check.

- If your students are a little more advanced, you might want to have them just work in twos or threes trying to decide which word from the pictures or reading list would fit in the space and make sense. Then when they have finished, they could correct their pages together as a whole group in consultation with you.

REVIEW VOCABULARY

These pages may be handled in one of several ways:

- Do as a group brainstorm as suggested for "Name It!" sections.

- Write all of the correct words on the blackboard in a scattered or random order. Students work in pairs to decide which words match which pictures and write them down.

- More advanced students might simply work together in twos or threes helping each other remember the labels and the spellings for each picture based on what they studied only.

- You might want to dictate the label for each picture within a sentence, using the page as a spelling and listening comprehension exercise.

Note: You will notice that sometimes the noun form of a word will appear in the picture cues in this section, while the verb form may appear in the pronunciation exercise below it. You may point out the difference if you feel it is of concern. However, parts of speech are not the focus here. Our objective is to emphasize recognition and pronunciation of consonant cluster endings such as (bz), (bd), (ps), (pt), (ts), (dz), (jd), (sh), (sht), (gz), and (gd).

Dictation and
Answer Key

Consonants

Page 46 – bcdf

Pictures

1. cab
2. bed
3. bee
4. food
5. cub
6. bib
7. cob
8. dad

Dictation

1. cod
2. bad
3. did
4. fad
5. dud
6. cuff
7. bead
8. dud
9. fed
10. cad
11. bid
12. dab
13. fid
14. cud
15. Bob

Page 47 – glmp

Pictures

1. leg
2. lip
3. log
4. mop
5. mug
6. pail
7. gum
8. pig

Dictation

1. gal
2. lad
3. mail
4. Pam
5. gull
6. lap
7. mom
8. pal
9. gag
10. map
11. pep
12. pull
13. lug
14. gap
15. dug

Page 48 – bcdfglmp – Review

Pictures

1. cap
2. dog
3. bug
4. cop
5. map
6. big
7. fall
8. bag

Dictation

1. pod
2. bad
3. fog
4. beam
5. cog
6. cam
7. beg
8. pup
9. fig
10. lad
11. pill
12. fad
13. pop
14. bum
15. dug

Page 49 – thsk

Pictures

1. sack
2. hat
3. kiss
4. seat
5. tack
6. kick
7. hit
8. sock

Dictation

1. hot
2. sick
3. kit
4. tick
5. sass
6. soot
7. tuck
8. toss
9. hack
10. hiss
11. sit
12. tot
13. hick
14. tat
15. hock

Page 50 – bcdfglmpthsk–Review

Pictures	Dictation	
1. bat	1. sad	9. cop
2. coat	2. cot	10. doff
3. pick	3. fit	11. lick
4. gas	4. Dick	12. get
5. milk	5. coal	13. bid
6. tag	6. dip	14. dock
7. back	7. ball	15. fast
8. pot	8. fist	

Page 51 – rjnv plus Review

Pictures	Dictation	
1. rug	1. jam	9. poor
2. run	2. vet	10. mar
3. van	3. van	11. pan
4. jet	4. nap	12. ton
5. jump	5. veil	13. John
6. vest	6. not	14. ruin
7. jar	7. ram	15. Jack
8. jug	8. vain	

Page 52 – qwxz plus Review

Pictures	Dictation	
1. six	1. quiz	9. win
2. web	2. wet	10. tax
3. queen	3. fix	11. wick
4. box	4. size	12. daze
5. zoo	5. wit	13. ax
6. fox	6. lax	14. whip
7. wall	7. gaze	15. quit
8. zip	8. quip	

Page 53 – Review

1. pin	5. lid	9. snail	13. belt
2. train	6. seal	10. tent	14. net
3. top	7. soap	11. meat	15. lamp
4. bus	8. tub	12. beet	16. nail

Page 54 – Review

1. robe	5. ham	9. nest	13. flag
2. fan	6. bean	10. sock	14. goat
3. rock	7. pick	11. drum	15. ax
4. feet	8. leaf	12. cot	16. suit

Page 55 – y – Two Sounds

Pictures	Dictation	
1. year	1. you	9. yam
2. pray	2. day	10. your
3. yell	3. try	11. yip
4. boy	4. ray	12. happy
5. yarn	5. yet	13. yellow
6. hay	6. may	14. play
7. yolk	7. yes	15. buy
8. day	8. pay	

Page 56 – g – Two Sounds

Pictures	Dictation	
1. log	1. got	9. beg
2. gun	2. age	10. tug
3. gem	3. gayle	11. good
4. garbage	4. dig	12. Gina
5. rug	5. Gene	13. gap
6. page	6. George	14. tag
7. gift	7. gum	15. rig
8. garage	8. gin	

Page 57 – c – Two Sounds

Pictures	Dictation	
1. clock	1. car	9. place
2. pencil	2. cop	10. candy
3. cup	3. like	11. Nancy
4. juice	4. city	12. nice
5. duck	5. pick	13. Coca-cola
6. ice cream	6. rice	14. Tracy
7. bicycle	7. dance	15. Cindy
8. sack	8. Lucy	

Page 58 – p and b Contrast

Pictures		Dictation	
1. cap	6. robe	1. peach	9. pole
2. cab	7. pea	2. bath	10. cob
3. pat	8. bee	3. pie	11. path
4. bat	9. pack	4. Bill	12. buy
5. rope	10. back	5. mop	13. bowl
		6. tab	14. cop
		7. beach	15. mob
		8. pill	

Page 59 – t and d Contrast

Pictures

1. seed	6. bet
2. seat	7. dime
3. beads	8. time
4. beets	9. dent
5. bed	10. tent

Dictation

1. tie	9. try
2. let	10. cart
3. had	11. hit
4. ten	12. hat
5. dry	13. led
6. den	14. dot
7. hid	15. card
8. die	

Page 60 – g and ck Contrast

Pictures

1. wig	6. pick
2. wick	7. bag
3. rag	8. back
4. rack	9. tag
5. pig	10. tack

Dictation

1. hag	9. bug
2. lack	10. shag
3. buck	11. shack
4. frog	12. lag
5. lug	13. wag
6. peg	14. frock
7. hack	15. peck
8. luck	

Page 61 – l and r Contrast

Pictures

1. lock	6. rip
2. rock	7. file
3. tile	8. fire
4. tire	9. lake
5. lip	10. rake

Dictation

1. lace	9. stole
2. dill	10. rash
3. loom	11. room
4. reap	12. store
5. leaf	13. race
6. lash	14. deer
7. tire	15. reef
8. leap	

Page 62 – j and h Contrast

Pictures

1. ham	6. jump
2. jam	7. hill
3. hug	8. Jill
4. jug	9. hay
5. hump	10. jay

Dictation

1. jail	9. jack
2. jaw	10. hello
3. he	11. jeer
4. jello	12. hail
5. had	13. joke
6. juice	14. jest
7. job	15. hear
8. hat	

Page 63 – v and w Contrast
Pictures

1. vest
2. west
3. veil
4. wail
5. v
6. we
7. viper
8. wiper
9. vet
10. wet

Dictation

1. very
2. we
3. vent
4. why
5. wiser
6. vie
7. vow
8. went
9. while
10. stow
11. stove
12. wary
13. vile
14. visor
15. wove

Page 64 – b and v Contrast
Pictures

1. bat
2. vat
3. boat
4. vote
5. best
6. vest
7. ban
8. van
9. curb
10. curve

Dictation

1. baby
2. vine
3. view
4. robe
5. stove
6. rave
7. boy
8. butter
9. love
10. valley
11. brown
12. mob
13. very
14. bottle
15. berry

Page 65 – sh and ch Contrast
Pictures

1. shoe
2. chew
3. sheep
4. cheap
5. wash
6. watch
7. cash
8. catch
9. shin
8. chin

Dictation

1. chair
2. chop
3. sheet
4. shin
5. shop
6. ditch
7. cheat
8. dish
9. cheese
10. wish
11. share
12. witch
13. she
14. chin
15. fish

Page 66 – ph and th Contrast
Pictures

1. elephant
2. telephone
3. thread
4. thin
5. photograph
6. pharmacy
7. teeth
8. three

Dictation

1. telegraph
2. alphabet
3. both
4. photograph
5. thank you
6. math
7. Phillip
8. thick
9. thumb
10. phrase
11. throw
12. think
13. graph
14. bath
15. with

Page 67 – Review

1. pen	9. nut
2. chop	10. fish
3. milk	11. chin
4. cot	12. hen
5. lamp	13. hat
6. pot	14. jet
7. fan	15. sun
8. bed	16. hair

Page 68 – Review

1. desk	9. snail
2. soap	10. pray
3. nail	11. three
4. fire	12. girl
5. drum	13. tub
6. bug	14. old
7. pie	15. feet
8. goat	16. brush

Page 69 – Review

1. ship	9. cap
2. clock	10. hill
3. cheese	11. top
4. belt	12. box
5. men	13. leaf
6. music	14. beard
7. suit	15. log
8. web	16. tree

Page 70 – Review

1. bell	9. block
2. nest	10. trunk
3. boy	11. beach
4. six	12. rocket
5. seal	13. peas
6. train	14. button
7. ruler	15. juice
8. fruit	16. truck

Vowels

Page 72	**Page 74**	**Page 77**	**Page 79**	**Page 82**
1. lamp	1. rake	1. ink	1. sign	1. net
2. bat	2. cane	2. lip	2. fight	2. pen
3. man	3. cake	3. sink	3. night	3. hen
4. cap	4. gate	4. ring	4. light	4. egg
5. ax	5. game	5. lid	5. fire	5. ten
6. pan	6. drapes	6. pick	6. five	6. nest
7. fan	7. grapes	7. dish	7. tire	7. bell
8. hat	8. plane	8. gift	8. bike	8. men
9. sack	9. snail	9. milk	9. kite	9. belt
10. back	10. nail	10. ship	10. stripe	10. vest
11. can	11. pail	11. fish	11. nine	11. tent
12. ham	12. train	12. chin	12. dime	12. leg
13. flag	13. hay	13. pin	13. line	13. bed
14. tag	14. May	14. hill	14. pie	14. desk
15. cat	15. pray	15. pig	15. tie	15. web
16. bag	16. tray	16. six	16. time	16. pencil

Page 84	**Page 87**	**Page 89**	**Page 92**	**Page 94**	**Page 97**
1. bee	1. top	1. rose	1. sun	1. cube	1. call
2. tree	2. spot	2. smoke	2. duck	2. tube	2. car
3. beet	3. clock	3. robe	3. jump	3. fuse	3. watch
4. feet	4. dog	4. stove	4. bus	4. ruler	4. ball
5. cheese	5. blocks	5. home	5. nut	5. pupil	5. walk
6. geese	6. fox	6. nose	6. cup	6. June	6. talk
7. needle	7. log	7. hose	7. jug	7. student	7. wall
8. three	8. rocket	8. rope	8. drum	8. music	8. water
9. bean	9. ox	9. cone	9. button	9. mule	9. tall
10. tea	10. lock	10. bone	10. tub	10. fumes	10. wash
11. meat	11. socks	11. toad	11. truck	11. juice	11. bar
12. seat	12. bottle	12. soap	12. bug	12. fruit	12. star
13. leaf	13. box	13. coat	13. gun	13. suit	13. cart
14. seal	14. rock	14. toast	14. brush	14. perfume	14. card
15. wheat	15. pot	15. boat	15. trunk	15. flute	15. park
16. peas	16. cot	16. goat	16. rug	16. glue	16. market

Initial Clusters

Page 120

Name it!
1. block
2. blonde
3. blow
4. blind
5. blade
6. blister
7. bloom
8. blood

Listen • Write • Read
1. black
2. blimp
3. block
4. blow
5. bloom
6. blonde
7. blisters
8. blade

Page 121

Name it!
1. bracelet
2. braid
3. branch
4. brush
5. bread
6. bridge
7. broken
8. breakfast

Listen • Write • Read
1. brave
2. bright
3. broom
4. brush
5. branch
6. braid
7. bracelet
8. bread

Page 122

Listen • Write
1. branch
2. blush
3. blue
4. bred
5. broom
6. blanch
7. brew
8. brush
9. bled
10. bloom
11. blade
12. braid

(Page 122 continued)
Listen · Write
1. bridge
2. brush
3. braid
4. blonde, brunette
5. branch, broken
6. blue, blanket

Page 123
Name it!
1. plug	3. plaid	5. plow	7. plump
2. plant	4. plane	6. plate	8. play

Listen · Write · Read
1. play
2. plate
3. plump
4. please
5. plant
6. plaid
7. plane
8. plug

Page 124
Name it!
1. price	3. prince	5. print	7. private
2. prize	4. present	6. prison	8. pray

Listen · Write · Read
1. present
2. private
3. prince
4. prison
5. print
6. pray
7. price
8. prize

Page 125
Listen • Write

1. plank	5. plum	9. problem
2. prow	6. prank	10. plow
3. pray	7. present	11. practice
4. pleasant	8. plastic	12. praise

Listen • Write
1. Prunes, plums
2. play
3. practice
4. plastic
5. plow
6. Please

Page 126
Review Vocabulary

1. bracelet	5. blister	9. price	13. bridge
2. prize	6. plant	10. branch	14. plaid
3. blade	7. prince	11. bloom	15. print
4. plug	8. braid	12. prison	16. blood

Page 127
Name it!

1. clover	3. clock	5. cliff	7. clip
2. closet	4. clamp	6. clothes	8. climb

Listen • Write • Read
1. clothes
2. closet
3. clover
4. cliff
5. clock
6. climb
7. clip
8. clamp

Page 128
Name it!
1. cricket
2. crown
3. cross
4. crayon
5. crib
6. crook
7. crab
8. cry

Listen · Write · Read
1. cry
2. crown
3. crayons
4. crab
5. cricket
6. crib
7. crook
8. Cross

Page 129
Listen · Write
1. crack
2. claw
3. class
4. crock
5. crash
6. clack
7. clouds
8. crass
9. crowds
10. clash
11. claw
12. clock

Listen · Write
1. class
2. crowd
3. clouds
4. claws
5. crash
6. clamp

Page 130
Name it!
1. glass
2. globe
3. glove
4. glue

Listen · Write · Read
1. gloves
2. glad
3. glass
4. globe
5. glance
6. gloss
7. glue
8. glaze

Page 131
Name it!
1. grapes
2. grandma/
   grandmother
3. grass
4. grain
5. grin
6. groom
7. gray
8. grow

Listen • Write • Read
1. grin
2. grass
3. grain
4. groom
5. Grapes
6. grow
7. grandmother
8. gray

Page 132
Listen • Write
1. grass
2. gloom
3. glue
4. gleam
5. graze
6. grade
7. groom
8. green
9. gloss
10. grew
11. glass
12. glaze

Listen • Write
1. grow
2. glue
3. grass, green
4. glass
5. grill
6. grade

Page 133
Review Vocabulary
1. glue
2. cry
3. cricket
4. clamp
5. clover
6. crown
7. grandma
8. globe
9. grass
10. closet
11. cross
12. grain
13. crayon
14. glass
15. grin
16. cliff

Page 134

Review Vocabulary

1. broom	9. plush	17. crown
2. crack	10. gloom	18. clack
3. play	11. clay	19. plate
4. glint	12. bran	20. breed
5. brown	13. blush	21. clown
6. plan	14. print	22. groom
7. crush	15. bloom	23. brush
8. greed	16. black	24. gray

Name it!

1. present	3. block	5. grapes	7. glove
2. crib	4. clock	6. brush	8. plane

Page 135

Name it!

1. flag	3. flashlight	5. flock	7. flower
2. flame	4. flea	6. flood	8. flute

Listen · Write · Read

1. flag
2. flame
3. flashlight
4. flea
5. flowers
6. flake
7. flute
8. flock

Page 136

Name it!

1. frog	3. flame	5. France	7. free
2. fruit	4. frying pan	6. freckles	8. friends

Listen · Write · Read

1. frying pan	5. fruit
2. friends	6. frog
3. freckles	7. free
4. France	8. frame

Page 137
Listen • Write

1. fresh	5. flame	9. frank
2. flank	6. flight	10. flute
3. fright	7. flesh	11. freight
4. fruit	8. freezer	12. front

Listen • Write
1. fresh
2. fruit
3. freezer
4. flute
5. front
6. free

Page 138
Name it!

1. train	3. trunk	5. trumpet	7. truck
2. tray	4. tree	6. trail	8. trap

Listen • Write • Read
1. tree
2. trunk
3. train
4. tray
5. trap
6. trunk
7. Trumpets
8. trail

Page 139
Name it!

1. drum	3. drive	5. drink	7. dream
2. drapes	4. drugs	6. dress	8. drain

(Page 139 continued)
Listen · Write · Read
1. dress
2. drink
3. drum
4. dream
5. drug
6. drive
7. Drapes
8. drain

Page 140
Listen · Write
1. trail
2. truck
3. dry
4. tree
5. dress
6. true
7. try
8. drop
9. trip
10. drip
11. drink
12. drapes

Listen · Write
1. tree
2. drive, truck
3. train
4. Dry
5. dress
6. draw

Page 141
Review Vocabulary
1. fruit
2. trunk
3. France
4. trap
5. free
6. flood
7. trail
8. friends
9. trumpet
10. tree
11. freckles
12. flea
13. flashlight
14. dream
15. truck
16. drugs

Page 142
Name it!
1. thin
2. thief
3. thank you
4. think
5. three
6. throat
7. throw
8. thread

Listen · Write · Read
1. thread
2. thin
3. three
4. think
5. thank
6. Throw
7. throat
8. thief

Page 143

Review Vocabulary

1. train	9. true	17. three
2. friends	10. draw	18. flag
3. flame	11. think	19. tray
4. drum	12. fruit	20. flame
5. thin	13. truck	21. dresser
6. truck	14. flute	22. drip
7. frog	15. drink	23. fly
8. thread	16. throat	24. thief

Name it!

1. train	3. dress	5. thin	7. flower
2. flag	4. frog	6. throat	8. frame

Page 144

Review Vocabulary

1. private	5. tray	9. drive	13. groom
2. plate	6. gray	10. blind	14. clip
3. blonde	7. frying pan	11. pray	15. drain
4. clothes	8. crab	12. drum	16. crook

Page 145

Name it!

1. spool	4. spill	7. spear	10. spray
2. spider	5. spade	8. spine	11. splash
3. sports	6. spot	9. spring	12. split

Listen · Write · Read
1. spool
2. sports
3. spiders
4. spill
5. Spray
6. splash
7. spots
8. spend

Page 146
Name it!

1. stove
2. student
3. stamp
4. stomach
5. steam
6. stage
7. stars
8. strike
9. straw
10. stripe
11. string
12. stream

Listen · Write · Read
1. stamp
2. stream
3. stomach
4. string
5. stars
6. steam
7. student
8. stand, stage

Page 147
Name it!

1. smile
2. smoke
3. small
4. smell
5. snake
6. sneeze
7. snore
8. snail
9. slow
10. slide
11. sled
12. sleep

Listen · Write · Read
1. smell, smoke
2. snail, slow
3. snore
4. Smile
5. small
6. slide
7. snake
8. sneeze

Page 148
Review Vocabulary

1. speak
2. spray
3. sting
4. small
5. string
6. straw
7. snow
8. slow
9. stay
10. snake

Page 149
Review Vocabulary

1. spool	5. strike	9. string	13. snake
2. small	6. spring	10. splash	14. sneeze
3. stamp	7. snore	11. slow	15. stove
4. straw	8. sports	12. smoke	16. spray

Page 150
Name it!

1. squint	4. squirrel	7. scarf	10. ski
2. square	5. scale	8. skirt	11. screw
3. squeeze	6. scar	9. skate	12. scratch

Listen · Write · Read

1. skate	5. skirt
2. square	6. scarf
3. Squeeze	7. ski
4. screw	8. scratch

Page 151
Review Vocabulary

1. stage	5. spots	9. square	13. student
2. spine	6. smile	10. ski	14. sleep
3. scale	7. squeeze	11. screw	15. spear
4. skate	8. stream	12. stars	16. snail

Page 152
Name it!

1. shoe	3. ship	5. shave	7. shrub
2. sheep	4. shower	6. shrimp	8. shrink

Listen · Write · Read

1. shoe	5. show
2. socks	6. shrub
3. shave, shower	7. sheep
4. socks, shrink	8. ship

Page 153
Review Vocabulary

1. scarf	5. grandma	9. cry	13. slide
2. bracelet	6. stomach	10. drapes	14. drain
3. blow	7. block	11. drink	15. braid
4. think	8. shave	12. steam	16. crab

Page 154
Review Vocabulary

1. shoe	5. plane	9. scar	13. blow
2. dream	6. flower	10. theif/crook	14. brush
3. spill	7. small	11. thank you	15. trumpet
4. print	8. blood	12. grass	16. squirrel

Page 155
Review Vocabulary

1. spade	5. squeeze	9. prize	13. smell
2. blade	6. sheep/flock	10. freckles	14. cricket
3. blind	7. clip	11. breakfast	15. pray
4. globe	8. three	12. grapes	16. ship

Page 156
Review Vocabulary

1. shrimp	5. spider	9. trap	13. shower
2. friends	6. spool/thread	10. price	14. strike
3. crayon	7. branch	11. bloom	15. glove
4. think	8. sled	12. plug	16. climb

Page 157
Review Vocabulary

1. sneeze	5. smoke	9. present	13. drive
2. string	6. crib	10. screw	14. clothes
3. plant	7. closet	11. shrink	15. free
4. scale	8. grass	12. France	16. bridge

Final Clusters

Page 160
Name it!
1. cab
2. tube
3. bib
4. cube
5. tub
6. web
7. ribs
8. robe

Listen • Write • Read
1. robbed
2. Cubs
3. cubes
4. rubbed
5. tubes
6. bibs

Page 161
Name it!
1. soap
2. mop
3. cap
4. ship
5. top
6. cup
7. slip
8. cop

Listen • Write • Read
1. maps
2. tapes
3. zipped
4. cups
5. mopped
6. typed

Page 162
Listen • Write
1. robs
2. fibbed
3. sobs
4. mapped
5. zips
6. soaps
7. keeps
8. rubbed
9. sleeps
10. ribs
11. mopped
12. rips

Listen • Write • Read
1. roped
2. Robs
3. Sobs
4. zipped
5. keeps
6. ribs

Page 163
Name it!
1. fruit
2. gate
3. rocket
4. cat
5. net
6. pot
7. light
8. hat
9. lid
10. ride
11. bed
12. seed
13. bread
14. kid
15. bead
16. road

Page 164
Listen · Write
1. cabs
2. maps
3. steps
4. robs
5. tubs
6. soups
7. beds
8. boots
9. lights
10. nets
11. roads
12. bids

Listen · Write · Read
1. mops
2. cups
3. rods
4. soups
5. beets
6. boots
7. beds

Page 165
Name it!
1. scratch
2. latch
3. hatch
4. match
5. watch
6. patch
7. beach
8. peach

Listen · Write · Read
1. patched
2. touched
3. hitched
4. watched
5. hatched
6. reached
7. scratched

Page 166
Name it!
1. huge
2. cage
3. page
4. badge
5. ledge
6. hedge
7. edge
8. sage

Listen · Write · Read
1. caged
2. badge
3. page
4. edge
5. sage
6. rage
7. hedge

Page 167
Name it!
1. fish
2. dish
3. cash
4. wash
5. push
6. crash

Listen · Write · Read
1. cashed
2. washed
3. crashed
4. fished
5. pushed
6. dished

Page 168
Listen · Write
1. watched
2. washed
3. pushed
4. caged
5. cashed
6. ditched
7. paged
8. crashed
9. dished
10. raged
11. hatched
12. hedged

Listen · Write · Read
1. watched
2. caged
3. reached
4. hatched
5. cashed
6. patched
7. pushed
8. washed

Page 169
Review Vocabulary
Name it!

1. hats	5. rides	9. pushed	13. tops
2. caged	6. crashed	10. seeds	14. nets
3. cubes	7. pots	11. hedge	15. beds
4. soaps	8. cups	12. tubes	16. washed

Page 170
Name it!

1. flag	3. bag	5. leg	7. pig
2. dog	4. bug	6. tag	8. dig

Listen · Write · Read
1. dogs
2. flags
3. legs
4. begged
5. tagged
6. jogs

Page 171
Name it!

1. lock	3. smoke	5. cheek	7. rock
2. block	4. black	6. rake	8. sock

Listen · Write · Read
1. picked
2. socks
3. checked
4. looks
5. raked
6. locked
7. smokes
8. books

Page 172
Name it!
1. fox
2. six
3. wax
4. box
5. mix
6. tax

Listen · Write · Read
1. mixed
2. boxed
3. waxed
4. text
5. Next
6. tax

Page 173
Listen · Write
1. tacked
2. bags
3. pecks
4. tagged
5. pegs
6. bagged
7. tags
8. backs
9. tacks
10. pegged
11. backed
12. pecked

Listen · Write · Read
1. tacked
2. pecked
3. tags
4. tacks
5. bags
6. tagged
7. Pegs
8. backed

Page 174
Name it!
1. chef
2. wave
3. knife
4. roof
5. leaf
6. love
7. five
8. dive

Page 175
Name it!
1. chefs
2. waved
3. knives
4. roofs
5. leaves
6. fives
7. dives
8. loved

Listen · Write · Read
1. Two chefs cooked the dinner.
2. Jack waved goodbye to Susan.
3. Two knives are on the table.
4. The roofs are brown.
5. In October the leaves fall from the trees.
6. She wrote two fives on her paper.
7. He swims and dives well.
8. He has loved her for 15 years.

Page 176

Name it!

1. belt	4. wilt	7. melt	10. bolt
2. old	5. child	8. colt	11. cold
3. hold	6. weld	9. salt	12. bald

Listen · Write · Read
1. salt
2. belts
3. child
4. old
5. bolts
6. holds
7. wilt

Page 177

Name it!

1. tire	3. share	5. pour	7. toaster
2. ruler	4. ladder	6. letter	8. star

Listen · Write · Read
1. letters
2. poured
3. tires
4. toasters
5. rulers
6. ladders
7. stars
8. share

Page 178

Name it!

1. bell	3. bottle	5. kettle	7. needle
2. nail	4. peel	6. hill	8. pail

(Page 178 continued)
Listen · Write · Read
1. hills
2. peeled
3. rolled
4. mailed
5. bottles
6. nails
7. called
8. bells

Page 179
Listen · Write
1. fired
2. filed
3. cars
4. peeled
5. stars
6. firs
7. peels
8. peers
9. peered

Listen · Write · Read
1. files
2. called
3. peels
4. card
5. calls
6. filed
7. cars

Page 180
Review Vocabulary
1. fires
2. peeled
3. hold
4. poured
5. bolts
6. cold
7. hills
8. wilt
9. nailed
10. rulers
11. tires
12. bells
13. weld
14. toasters
15. needles
16. old
* Use in sentence for dictation

Page 181
1. heart
2. cart
3. card
4. yard
5. herd
6. hurt
7. guard
8. fort
9. bird
10. court
11. board
12. sword

(Page 181 continued)
Listen · Write · Read
1. cards
2. cart
3. courts
4. birds
5. hearts

Page 182
Name it!
1. pearl   3. girl   5. curl
2. world   4. squirrel   6. barrel

Listen · Write · Read
1. curls
2. barrels
3. girls
4. squirrels
5. pearls

Page 183
Name it!
1. surf   3. wharf   5. serve
2. scarf   4. curve   6. carve

Listen · Write · Read
1. scarves
2. curved
3. wharf
4. served
5. carves

Page 184
Review Vocabulary
1. curled   5. cards   9. served   13. barrels
2. scarves   6. squirrels   10. hearts   14. fort
3. cart   7. yard   11. world   15. curved
4. boards   8. girl   12. wharf   16. bird

Use in sentence for dictation

Page 185
Name it!
1. arm
2. barn
3. worm
4. yarn
5. storm
6. warm
7. burn
8. torn

Listen · Write · Read
1. burned, arms
2. torn
3. worms
4. yarn
5. barn
6. warms

Page 186
Name it!
1. charge
2. scorch
3. large
4. march
5. perch
6. church
7. torch
8. porch

Listen · Write · Read
1. marched
2. perched
3. search
4. searched
5. charge
6. March
7. enlarged
8. large

Page 187
Name it!
1. curb
2. herb
3. verbs
4. harp
5. sharp
6. chirp

Listen · Write · Read
1. herbs
2. verbs
3. harp
4. chirped
5. curb
6. sharp

Page 188
Name it!
1. purse
3. horse
5. thirst
7. burst
2. verse
4. nurse
6. first

Listen · Write · Read
1. nurse
4. first
2. burst
5. verse
3. purse
6. nursed

Page 189
Name it!
1. bark
2. park
3. work
4. mark

Listen · Write · Read
1. barked
5. works
2. bark
6. marked
3. park
7. parked
4. worked

Page 190
Review Vocabulary
1. arm
5. torch
9. barns
13. guard
2. church
6. herb
10. herd
14. harps
3. stormed
7. worms
11. warmed
15. court
4. large
8. chirped
12. perched
16. burned
* Use in sentence for dictation

Page 191
Review Vocabulary
1. edge
5. crash
9. cat
13. shipped
2. cap
6. cake
10. robed
14. pearl
3. rakes
7. gate
11. kettle
15. march
4. bibbed
8. digs
12. page
16. locked
* Use in sentence for dictation

Page 192
Review Vocabulary

1. ledge	5. black	9. child	13. leg
2. rockets	6. torn	10. badge	14. fished
3. cab	7. flag	11. boxed	15. sword
4. kite	8. ribs	12. lights	16. cash

* Use in sentence for dictation

Page 193
Review Vocabulary
Name it!

1. smokes	5. lid	9. squirrel	13. bagged
2. fruit	6. taxed	10. colt	14. tub
3. cheese	7. slip	11. cop	15. mixed
4. webbed	8. dog	12. belts	16. waved

Page 194
Name it!

1. dent	3. wind	5. pint	7. paint
2. hand	4. bent	6. tent	8. band

Listen · Write · Read
1. pants
2. band
3. paints
4. hands
5. pints
6. lands
7. bend

Page 195
Name it!

1. beans	4. button	7. pin	10. sign
2. gun	5. chicken	8. cane	11. pen
3. cone	6. bone	9. fan	12. ten

(Page 195 continued)
Listen · Write · Read
1. buttoned
2. pinned
3. beans
4. fans

Page 196
Name it!

1. ham	3. comb	5. room	7. climb
2. dime	4. home	6. lamb	8. dome

Listen · Write · Read
1. combed
2. climbed
3. rooms
4. dimes
5. homes
6. lambs

Page 197
Name it!

1. jump	2. stamp	3. lamp	4. camp	5. pump

Listen · Write · Read
1. stamps
2. stamped
3. jumped
4. camped
5. camps
6. pumps

Page 198

Name it!
1. bench	3. bunch	5. sponge	7. punch
2. wrench	4. lunch	6. hinge	8. change

Listen · Write · Read
1. bench	4. lunch
2. sponge	5. change
3. hinge	6. changed

Page 199

Name it!
1. ring	3. junk	5. sing
2. ink	4. sink	6. swing

Listen · Write · Read
1. rings	4. sings
2. junk	5. swings
3. sinks	

Page 200

Review Vocabulary
1. beans	5. pinned	9. pint	13. lamp
2. band	6. hands	10. bent	14. junk
3. tens	7. sings	11. comb	15. stamp
4. wind	8. paints	12. camps	16. buttoned

Use in sentence for dictation

Page 201

Review Vocabulary
1. barked	5. signs	9. axed	13. melts
2. bottled	6. pen	10. dives	14. fox
3. swing	7. cones	11. homes	15. ring
4. rock	8. tent	12. sink	16. arm

Use in sentence for dictation

Page 202
Review Vocabulary

1. tagged	5. jumped	9. socks	13. inked
2. ox	6. chickens	10. pigs	14. pails
3. dimes	7. bones	11. yarn	15. fanned
4. bald	8. ladders	12. child	16. six

Page 203
Name it!

1. desk	2. disc	3. mask	4. tusk

Listen · Write · Read
1. ask
2. asked
3. masks
4. tusks
5. desk
6. masked
7. disc

Page 204
Name it!

1. waste	3. chest	5. paste	7. feast
2. nest	4. wrist	6. list	8. vest

Listen · Write · Read
1. list
2. wrist
3. nests
4. feast
5. vest
6. chest
7. Paste
8. waste

Page 205
Name it!
1. size
2. rose
3. nose
4. raise
5. buzz
6. hose

Listen · Write · Read
1. raised
2. buzzed
3. sizes
4. closed
5. closes
6. roses
7. hoses

Page 206
Review Vocabulary
1. desks
2. list
3. masked
4. wrist
5. tusks
6. waste
7. vests
8. washed
9. nests
10. push
11. disc
12. paste
13. fished
14. buzzed
15. crashed
16. dish

Page 207
Name it!
1. moth
2. bath
3. path
4. north
5. south
6. mouth

Listen · Write · Read
1. paths
2. baths
3. moths
4. mouths
5. south

Section One: Consonants

(Photocopiable Exercises)

bcdf

Name   **Sound**

1._____   5._____   1._____   5._____

2._____   6._____   2._____   6._____

3._____   7._____   3._____   7._____

4._____   8._____   4._____   8._____

1. ___ a ___

2. ___ e ___

3. ___ ee

4. ___ oo ___

5. ___ u ___

6. ___ i ___

7. ___ o ___

8. ___ a ___

1. ___ o ___   6. ___ uf ___   11. ___ i ___

2. ___ a ___   7. ___ ea ___   12. ___ a ___

3. ___ i ___   8. ___ u ___   13. ___ i ___

4. ___ a ___   9. ___ e ___   14. ___ u ___

5. ___ u ___   10. ___ a ___   15. ___ o ___

glmp

Name   **Sound**

1._____   5._____   1._____   5._____

2._____   6._____   2._____   6._____

3._____   7._____   3._____   7._____

4._____   8._____   4._____   8._____

1. __ e __

2. __ i __

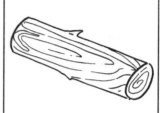

3. __ o __

4. __ o __

5. __ u __

6. __ ai __

7. __ u __

8. __ i __

1. __ a __   6. __ a __   11. __ e __

2. __ a __   7. __ o __   12. __ ul __

3. __ ai __   8. __ a __   13. __ u __

4. __ a __   9. __ a __   14. __ a __

5. __ ul __   10. __ a __   15. __ u __

Review

b c d f g l m p

Name   **Sound**

1._____   5._____   1._____   5._____

2._____   6._____   2._____   6._____

3._____   7._____   3._____   7._____

4._____   8._____   4._____   8._____

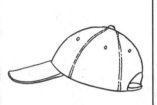

1. __ a __

2. __ o __

3. __ u __

4. __ o __

5. __ a __

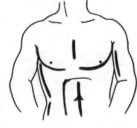

6. __ i __

7. __ a __

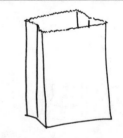

8. __ a __

1. __ o __   6. __ a __   11. __ il __

2. __ a __   7. __ e __   12. __ a __

3. __ o __   8. __ u __   13. __ o __

4. __ ea __   9. __ i __   14. __ u __

5. __ o __   10. __ a __   15. __ u __

thsk

Name   **Sound**

1._____   5._____   1._____   5._____

2._____   6._____   2._____   6._____

3._____   7._____   3._____   7._____

4._____   8._____   4._____   8._____

1. __ ac __   2. __ a __   3. __ i __ __   4. __ ea __

5. __ ac __   6. __ i __ __   7. __ i __   8. __ oc __

1. __ o __   6. __ oo __   11. __ i __

2. __ ic __   7. __ uc __   12. __ o __

3. __ i __   8. __ os __   13. __ ic __

4. __ ic __   9. __ ac __   14. __ a __

5. __ as __   10. __ is __   15. __ oc __

Review
b c d f g l m p t h s k

Name		Sound	
1._____	5._____	1._____	5._____
2._____	6._____	2._____	6._____
3._____	7._____	3._____	7._____
4._____	8._____	4._____	8._____

1. ___ a ___	2. ___ oa ___	3. ___ ic ___	4. ___ a ___
5. ___ i ___	6. ___ a ___	7. ___ ac ___	8. ___ o ___

1. ___ a ___	6. ___ i ___	11. ___ ic ___
2. ___ o ___	7. ___ al ___	12. ___ e ___
3. ___ i ___	8. ___ i ___	13. ___ i ___
4. ___ ic ___	9. ___ o ___	14. ___ oc ___
5. ___ oa ___	10. ___ of ___	15. ___ a ___ ___

rjnv plus Review

Name		Sound	
1._____	5._____	1._____	5._____
2._____	6._____	2._____	6._____
3._____	7._____	3._____	7._____
4._____	8._____	4._____	8._____

1. __ u __

2. __ u __

3. __ a __

4. __ e __

5. __ um __

6. __ es __

7. __ a __

8. __ u __

1. __ a __	6. __ o __	11. __ a __
2. __ e __	7. __ a __	12. __ o __
3. __ a __	8. __ ai __	13. __ oh __
4. __ a __	9. __ oo __	14. __ ui __
5. __ ei __	10. __ a __	14. __ 'ac __

qwxz plus Review

Name   **Sound**

1. _____   5. _____   1. _____   5. _____

2. _____   6. _____   2. _____   6. _____

3. _____   7. _____   3. _____   7. _____

4. _____   8. _____   4. _____   8. _____

  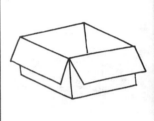

1. __ i __   2. __ e __   3. __ uee __   4. __ o __

5. ____ oo   6. __ o __   7. __ al __   8. __ i __

1. __ ui __   6. __ a __   11. __ ic __

2. __ e __   7. __ a __ e   12. __ a __ e

3. __ i __   8. __ ui __   13. a __

4. __ i __ e   9. __ i __   14. __ hi __

5. __ i __   10. __ a __   15. __ ui __

Review

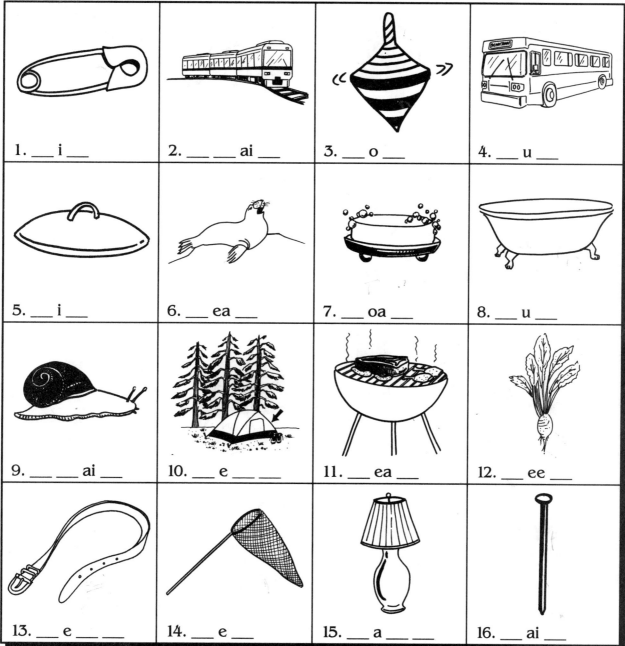

1. __ i __

2. __ __ ai __

3. __ o __

4. __ u __

5. __ i __

6. __ ea __

7. __ oa __

8. __ u __

9. __ __ ai __

10. __ e __ __ __

11. __ ea __

12. __ ee __

13. __ e __ __ __

14. __ e __

15. __ a __ __ __

16. __ ai __

Review

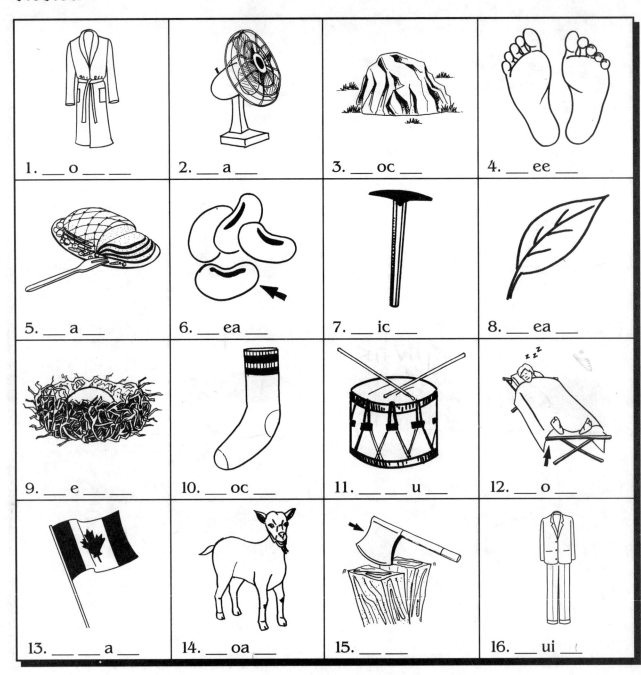

1. __ o __ __

2. __ a __

3. __ oc __

4. __ ee __

5. __ a __

6. __ ea __

7. __ ic __

8. __ ea __

9. __ e __ __

10. __ oc __

11. __ __ u __

12. __ o __

13. __ __ a __

14. __ oa __

15. __ __ __

16. __ ui __

Sounds Easy!©2002 Alta Book Center Publishers, San Francisco, California
Permission granted to photocopy for one teacher's classroom use only.

Sound 1

b a b <u>y</u>

Sound 2

<u>y</u> o u

y

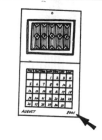

1. ___ ea ___

2. ___ ___ a ___

3. ___ el ___

4. ___ o ___

5. ___ a ___ ___ ___

6. ___ ___ a ___

7. ___ ol ___

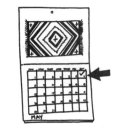

8. ___ a ___

1. ___ ou

2. ___ a ___

3. ___ r ___

4. ___ a ___

5. ___ e ___

6. ___ a ___

7. ___ e ___

8. ___ a ___

9. ___ a ___

10. ___ ou ___

11. ___ i ___

12. ___ ap ___ ___

13. ___ el ___ ow

14. ___ ___ a ___

15. ___ u ___

Sound 1

g a s o l i n e

Sound 2

o r a n <u>g</u> e

g

1. __ o __	2. __ u __	3. __ e __	4. __ a __ __ a __ e
6. __ u __	6. __ __ a __ e	7. __ i __ __	8. __ __ a __ a __ e

1. __ o __	6. __ eo __ __ e	11. __ oo __
2. a __ e	7. __ u __	12. __ i __ a
3. __ ay __ e	8. __ i __	13. __ a __
4. __ i __	9. __ e __	14. __ a __
5. __ e __ e	10. __ u __	15. __ i __

Sound 1

c i t y

Sound 2

c a n

C

1. ___ ___ o ___ k

2. ___ e ___ ___ i ___

3. ___ u ___

4. ___ ui ___ e

5. ___ u ___ k

6. i ___ e ___ rea ___

7. ___ i ___ y ___ le

8. ___ a ___ k

1. ___ ar ___

2. ___ o ___

3. ___ i ___ e

4. ___ i ___ y

5. ___ i ___ k

6. ___ i ___ e

7. ___ a ___ ___ e

8. ___ u ___ y

9. ___ ___ a ___ e

10. ___ a ___ dy

11. ___ a ___ ___ y

12. ___ i ___ e

13. ___ o ___ a- ___ o ___ a

14. ___ ___ a ___ y

15. ___ i ___ ___ y

p   **b**

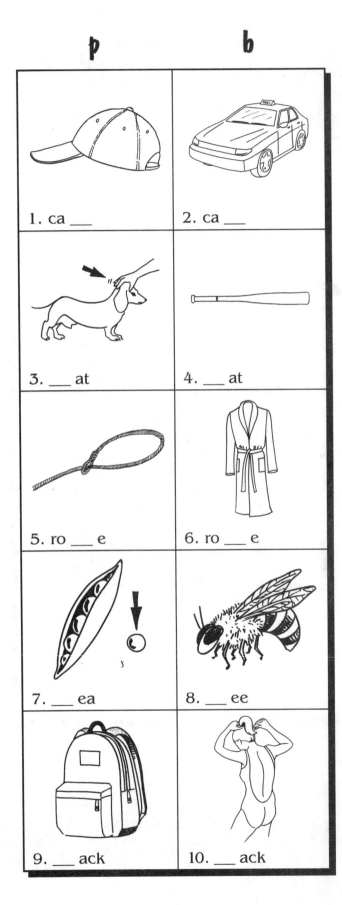

1. ca ___

2. ca ___

3. ___ at

4. ___ at

5. ro ___ e

6. ro ___ e

7. ___ ea

8. ___ ee

9. ___ ack

10. ___ ack

p·b

1. ___ each

2. ___ ath

3. ___ ie

4. ___ ill

5. mo ___

6. ta ___

7. ___ each

8. ___ ill

9. ___ ole

10. co ___

11. ___ ath

12. ___ uy

13. ___ owl

14. co ___

15. mo ___

d   t

d·t

1. see ___	2. sea ___
3. bea ___ s	4. bee ___ s
5. be ___	6. be ___
7. ___ ime	8. ___ ime
9. ___ en ___	10. ___ en ___

1. ___ ie

2. le ___

3. ha ___

4. ___ en

5. ___ ry

6. ___ en

7. hi ___

8. ___ ie

9. ___ ry

10. car ___

11. hi ___

12. ha ___

13. le ___

14. ___ ot

15. car ___

g	**ck**

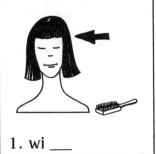

1. wi ___

2. wi ___ ___

3. ra ___

4. ra ___ ___

5. pi ___

6. pi ___ ___

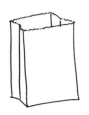

7. ba ___

8. ba ___ ___

9. ta ___

10. ta ___ ___

g·ck

1. ha ___

2. la ___ ___

3. bu ___ ___

4. fro ___

5. lu ___

6. pe ___

7. ha ___ ___

8. lu ___ ___

9. bu ___

10. sha ___

11. sha ___ ___

12. la ___

13. wa ___

14. fro ___ ___

15. pe ___ ___

l   **r**

l·r

l	r
1. ___ ock	2. ___ ock
3. ti ___ e	4. ti ___ e
5. ___ ip	6. ___ ip
7. fi ___ e	8. fi ___ e
9. ___ ake	10. ___ ake

1. ___ ace

2. di ___ ___

3. ___ oom

4. ___ eap

5. ___ eaf

6. ___ ash

7. ti ___ e

8. ___ eap

9. sto ___ e

10. ___ ash

11. ___ oom

12. sto ___ e

13. ___ ace

14. dee ___

15. ___ eef

h   j

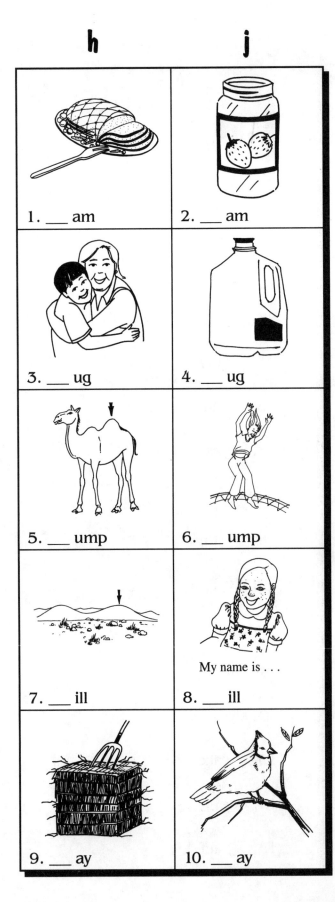

1. ___ am
2. ___ am
3. ___ ug
4. ___ ug
5. ___ ump
6. ___ ump
7. ___ ill
8. ___ ill

My name is . . .

9. ___ ay
10. ___ ay

h·j

1. ___ ail
2. ___ aw
3. ___ e
4. ___ ello
5. ___ ad
6. ___ uice
7. ___ ob
8. ___ at
9. ___ ack
10. ___ ello
11. ___ eer
12. ___ ail
13. ___ oke
14. ___ est
15. ___ ear

V   W

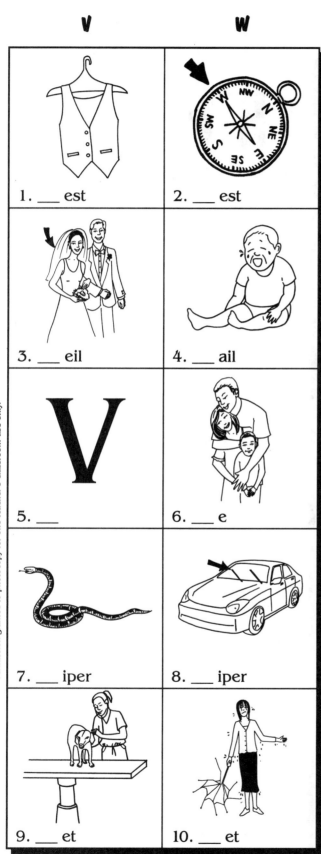

1. ___ est

2. ___ est

3. ___ eil

4. ___ ail

5. ___

6. ___ e

7. ___ iper

8. ___ iper

9. ___ et

10. ___ et

V·W

1. ___ ery

2. ___ e

3. ___ ent

4. ___ hy

5. ___ iser

6. ___ ie

7. ___ ow

8. ___ ent

9. ___ hile

10. sto ___

11. sto ___ e

12. ___ ary

13. ___ ile

14. ___ isor

15. ___ o ___ e

b	v
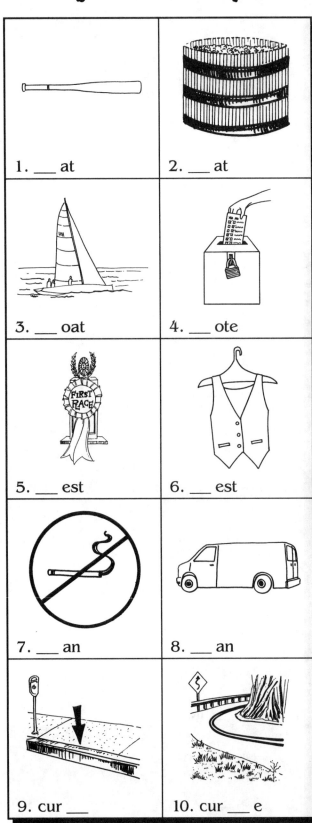 1. ___ at	2. ___ at
3. ___ oat	4. ___ ote
5. ___ est	6. ___ est
7. ___ an	8. ___ an
9. cur ___	10. cur ___ e

b·v

1. ___ a ___ y

2. ___ ine

3. ___ iew

4. ro ___ e

5. sto ___ e

6. ra ___ e

7. ___ oy

8. ___ utter

9. lo ___ e

10. ___ alley

11. ___ rown

12. mo ___

13. ___ ery

14. ___ ottle

15. ___ erry

sh   ch

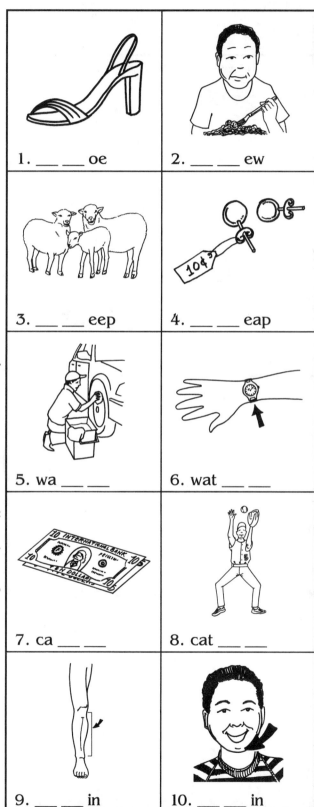

1. ___ ___ oe

2. ___ ___ ew

3. ___ ___ eep

4. ___ ___ eap

5. wa ___ ___

6. wat ___ ___

7. ca ___ ___

8. cat ___ ___

9. ___ ___ in

10. ___ ___ in

sh·ch

1. ___ ___ air

2. ___ ___ op

3. ___ ___ eet

4. ___ ___ in

5. ___ ___ op

6. dit ___ ___

7. ___ ___ eat

8. di ___ ___

9. ___ ___ eese

10. wi ___ ___

11. ___ ___ are

12. wit ___ ___

13. ___ ___ e

14. ___ ___ in

15. fi ___ ___

ph·th

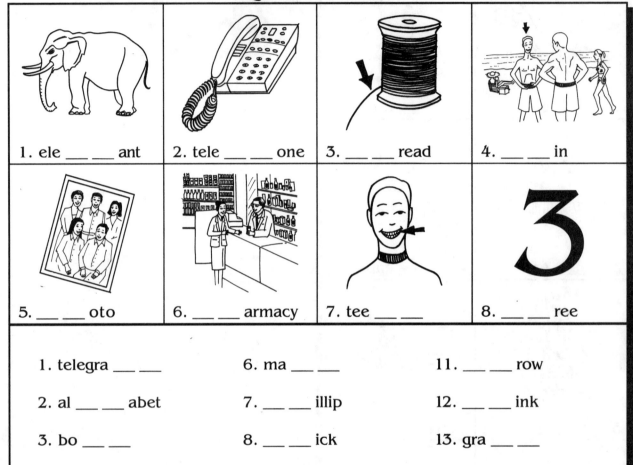

1. ele __ __ ant
2. tele __ __ one
3. __ __ read
4. __ __ in
5. __ __ oto
6. __ __ armacy
7. tee __ __
8. __ __ ree

1. telegra __ __
2. al __ __ abet
3. bo __ __
4. __ __ onogra __ __
5. __ __ ank you

6. ma __ __
7. __ __ illip
8. __ __ ick
9. __ __ umb
10. __ __ rase

11. __ __ row
12. __ __ ink
13. gra __ __
14. ba __ __
15. wi __ __

Review

1. __ e __

2. __ __ o __

3. __ i __ __

4. __ o __

5. __ a __ __

6. __ o __

7. __ a __

8. __ e __

9. __ u __

10. __ i __ __ __

11. __ __ i __

12. __ e __

13. __ a __

14. __ e __

15. __ u __

16. __ ai __

Review

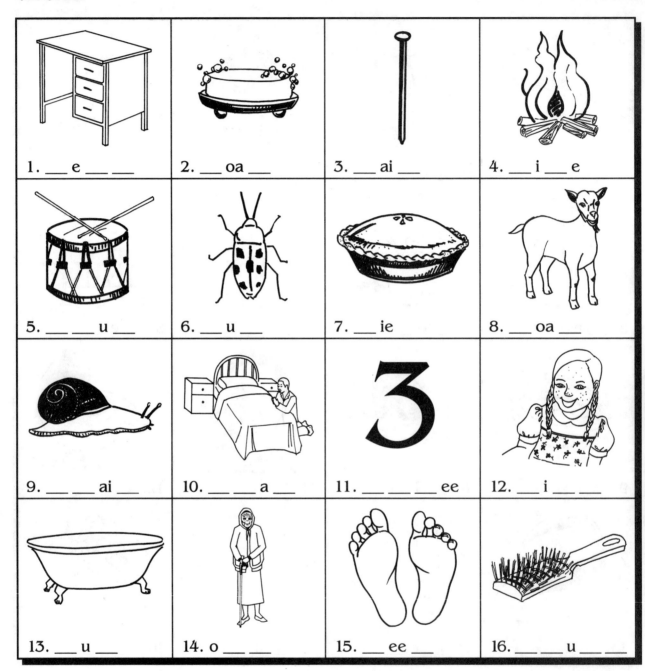

1. __ e __ __

2. __ oa __

3. __ ai __

4. __ i __ e

5. __ __ u __

6. __ u __

7. __ ie

8. __ oa __

9. __ __ ai __

10. __ __ a __

11. __ __ __ ee

12. __ i __ __ __

13. __ u __

14. o __ __ __

15. __ ee __

16. __ __ u __ __

Sounds Easy!©2002 Alta Book Center Publishers, San Francisco, California
Permission granted to photocopy for one teacher's classroom use only.

Review

1. __ __ i __

2. __ __ o __ __

3. __ __ ee __ __

4. __ e __ __

5. __ e __

6. __ u __ i __

7. __ ui __

8. __ e __

9. __ a __

10. __ i __ __

11. __ o __

12. __ o __

13. __ ea __

14. __ ea __ __

15. __ o __

16. __ __ ee

Review

1. __ e __ __ __

2. __ e __ __ __

3. __ o __

4. __ i __

5. __ ea __

6. __ __ ai __ __

7. __ u __ e

8. __ __ ui __

9. __ __ __ oc __

10. __ __ __ u __ __ __

11. __ ea __ __ __

12. __ oc __ e __

13. __ ea __

14. __ u __ o __ __

15. __ ui __ e

16. __ __ uc __

Section Two: Vowels

(Photocopiable Exercises)

Read

am	fat	pan
at	gas	ran
as	had	sad
bad	jam	sack
can	mad	happy
cap	map	tack
dad	pad	van

Write

1. _____
2. _____
3. _____
4. _____
5. _____
6. _____
7. _____
8. _____
9. _____
10. _____
11. _____
12. _____

Troublemakers

what	many
was	any

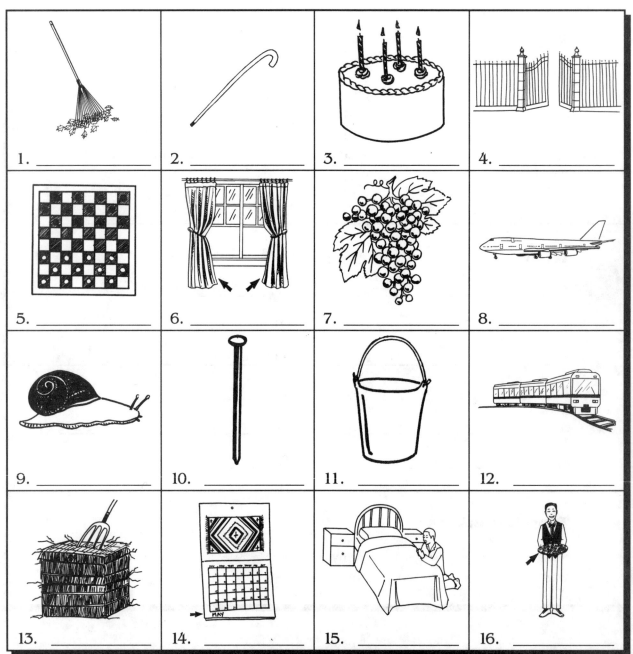

1. _____

2. _____

3. _____

4. _____

5. _____

6. _____

7. _____

8. _____

9. _____

10. _____

11. _____

12. _____

13. _____

14. _____

15. _____

16. _____

Spelling patterns for a

a

a • e	ai	ay

Read

ate	aid	day
bake	bait	hay
cape	chain	jay
face	maid	pay
game	mail	play
gave	pain	say
lane	rain	stay
make	train	tray

Write

1. _____   7. _____

2. _____   8. _____

3. _____   9. _____

4. _____   10. _____

5. _____   11. _____

6. _____   12. _____

Troublemakers

have	said	again
are	says	

a

a

Compare two sounds of a

man	sad	main	tape
pad	fat	pay	paid
lack	mad	made	rain
ran	tap	lake	fail
hat	pal	say	hay

Write

1. _____   7. _____

2. _____   8. _____

3. _____   9. _____

4. _____   10. _____

5. _____   11. _____

6. _____   12. _____

Read

Make a hat.   The rain came today.   Play the tape.
A man paid.   A cat ran.   Sam is fat.

Sounds Easy!©2002 Alta Book Center Publishers, San Francisco, California
Permission granted to photocopy for one teacher's classroom use only.

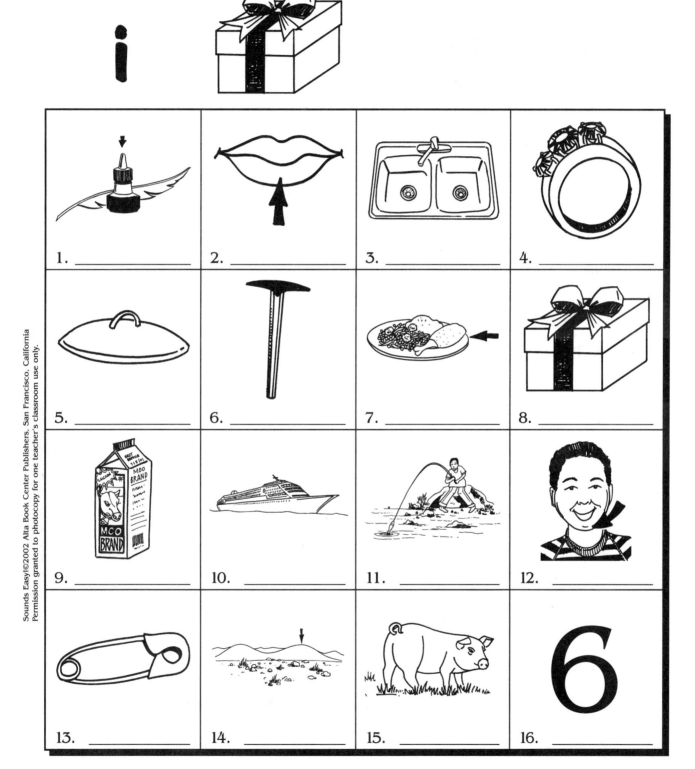

1. _____
2. _____
3. _____
4. _____
5. _____
6. _____
7. _____
8. _____
9. _____
10. _____
11. _____
12. _____
13. _____
14. _____
15. _____
16. _____

i

Read

is	him	pin	window
it	his	rim	will
in	kick	sit	zip
big	mitt	sip	
bit	kitchen	six	
did	pick	thin	
fin	pig	this	

Write

1. _____   7. _____

2. _____   8. _____

3. _____   9. _____

4. _____   10. _____

5. _____   11. _____

6. _____   12. _____

Troublemakers

hi
find

1. _____

2. _____

3. _____

4. _____

5. _____

6. _____

7. _____

8. _____

9. _____

10. _____

11. _____

12. _____

13. _____

14. _____

15. _____

16. _____

1:30 pm

Spelling patterns for i

i • e   ie   igh

Read

I	mile	pie	fight
bike	mine	tie	sight
dime	nine	lie	tight
drive	ride		might
fine	size		
five	smile		
like	time		
line	white		

Write

1. _____   7. _____

2. _____   8. _____

3. _____   9. _____

4. _____   10. _____

5. _____   11. _____

6. _____   12. _____

Troublemakers

piece   field
believe   friend

Sounds Easy!©2002 Alta Book Center Publishers, San Francisco, California
Permission granted to photocopy for one teacher's classroom use only.

Compare two sounds of i

bid	sit	like	hide
bit	sin	sight	light
lit	win	tile	bite
hid	till	bide	sign
kit	lick	kite	wine

Write

1. _____   7. _____

2. _____   8. _____

3. _____   9. _____

4. _____   10. _____

5. _____   11. _____

6. _____   12. _____

Read

Sit in the window.   Hide his bike.

I like it.   I lit the light.

Is this the kithcen?

Sounds Easy!©2002 Alta Book Center Publishers, San Francisco, California
Permission granted to photocopy for one teacher's classroom use only.

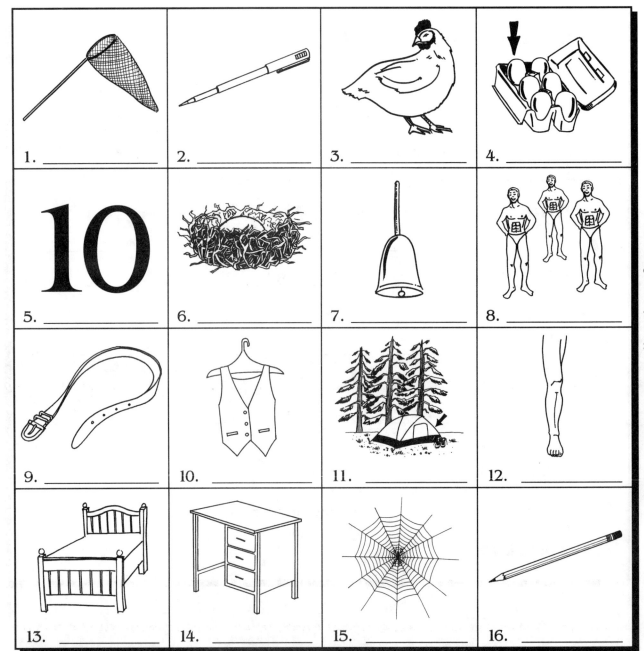

1. _____

2. _____

3. _____

4. _____

5. _____

6. _____

7. _____

8. _____

9. _____

10. _____

11. _____

12. _____

13. _____

14. _____

15. _____

16. _____

Read

Ed	men	yellow
bed	net	yes
egg	pep	yet
fell	red	elephant
get	sell	bell
jet	ten	them
leg	web	best
letter	well	hello

Write

1. _____
2. _____
3. _____
4. _____
5. _____
6. _____

7. _____
8. _____
9. _____
10. _____
11. _____
12. _____

Troublemakers

they	we	she
the	he	me

e

1. _____ 2. _____ 3. _____ 4. _____

5. _____ 6. _____ 7. _____ 8. _____

9. _____ 10. _____ 11. _____ 12. _____

13. _____ 14. _____ 15. _____ 16. _____

Spelling patterns for e

e

ee   ea

Read

free	feel	flea	please
see	green	pea	cream
three	keep	sea	mean
tree	meet	tea	peach
beef	need	eat	read
cheek	sheep	beach	speak
cheese	sleep	cheap	teacher
feed	teeth	clean	weak

Write

1. _____   7. _____

2. _____   8. _____

3. _____   9. _____

4. _____   10. _____

5. _____   11. _____

6. _____   12. _____

Read

head	been	great	ocean
bread		steak	beautiful
thread		break	
instead			
dead			

e

e

Compare two sounds of e

bed	fell	weed	bead
bet	men	beat	feed
den	peck	feel	reed
fed	sell	dean	mean
red	wed	peek	seal

Write

1. _____   7. _____

2. _____   8. _____

3. _____   9. _____

4. _____   10. _____

5. _____   11. _____

6. _____   12. _____

Read

I see seven men.

He sells beads.

She sleeps in the best bed.

Three sheep eat weeds.

Do elephants eat peas and eggs?

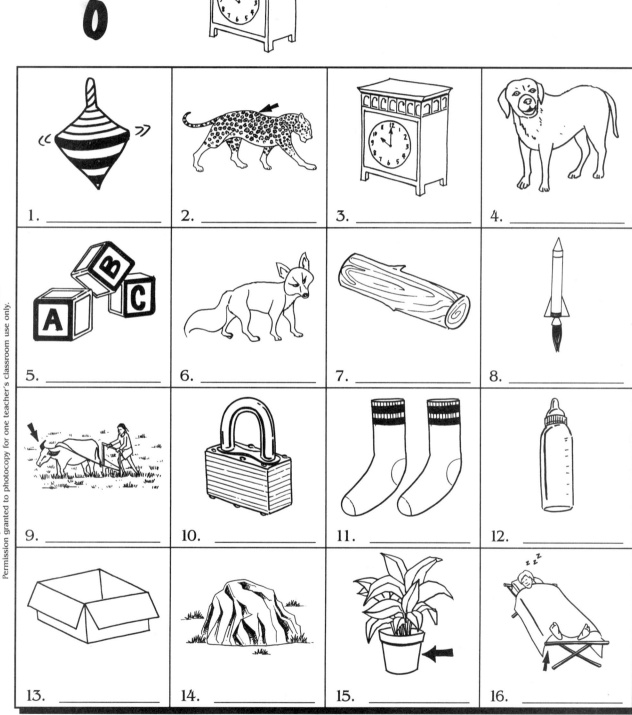

1. _____

2. _____

3. _____

4. _____

5. _____

6. _____

7. _____

8. _____

9. _____

10. _____

11. _____

12. _____

13. _____

14. _____

15. _____

16. _____

0

Read

Bob	mop	dot
box	not	fog
cot	on	hog
doll	off	jog
got	rod	lock
hot	top	block
job	tot	nod
lot	cob	rob

Write

1. _____
2. _____
3. _____
4. _____
5. _____
6. _____
7. _____
8. _____
9. _____
10. _____
11. _____
12. _____

Troublemakers

go	do	most	color
so	who	both	doctor
	you	only	young
			cousin
			country

1. _____
2. _____
3. _____
4. _____
5. _____
6. _____
7. _____
8. _____
9. _____
10. _____
11. _____
12. _____
13. _____
14. _____
15. _____
16. _____

Spelling patterns for o

o

oe	ow	o • e	oa

Read

toe	mow	broke	cloak
Joe	low	close	coal
hoe	throw	dome	foam
woe	blow	drove	groan
		hole	load
		joke	road
		lone	soap
		nose	toast

Write

1. _____ 7. _____

2. _____ 8. _____

3. _____ 9. _____

4. _____ 10. _____

5. _____ 11. _____

6. _____ 12. _____

Troublemakers

love	some	prove	gone
done	one	move	women
come	does	lose	
none		shoe	

o

o

Compare two sounds of o

cop	sop	soak	code
cod	mop	robe	road
cot	not	dole	mope
doll	rob	coat	note
rob	sock	cope	soap

Write

1. _____

2. _____

3. _____

4. _____

5. _____

6. _____

7. _____

8. _____

9. _____

10. _____

11. _____

12. _____

Read

Jon broke the clock.
The socks are in the box.
Bob got a coat.

Don't throw the soap.
Tom drove on an old road.

u

1. _____	2. _____	3. _____	4. _____
5. _____	6. _____	7. _____	8. _____
9. _____	10. _____	11. _____	12. _____
13. _____	14. _____	15. _____	16. _____

Sounds Easy!©2002 Alta Book Center Publishers, San Francisco, California
Permission granted to photocopy for one teacher's classroom use only.

u

Read

us	jut	under
up	mutt	umbrella
bud	nun	understand
bun	pup	truck
cut	rub	sun
duck	sum	dug
gum	run	study
hug	dull	bucket

Write

1. _____   7. _____

2. _____   8. _____

3. _____   9. _____

4. _____   10. _____

5. _____   11. _____

6. _____   12. _____

Troublemakers

bull	usual	put	busy
full	human		business
pull			

u

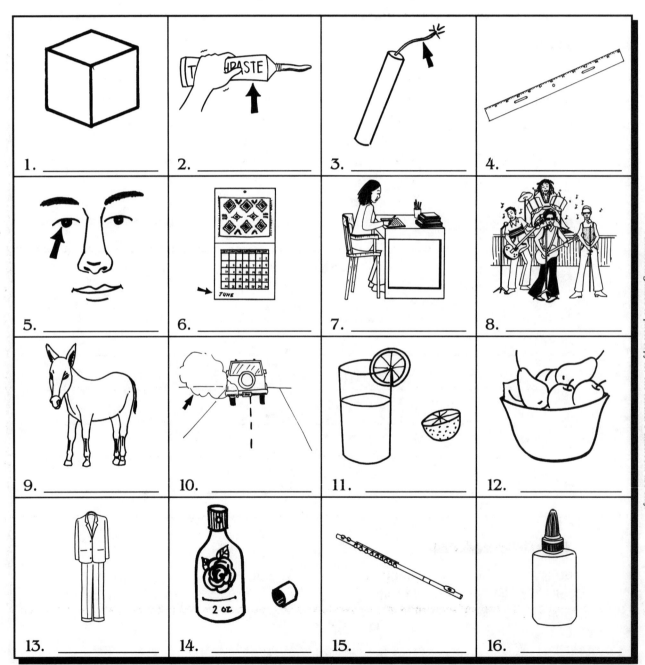

1. _____ 2. _____ 3. _____ 4. _____

5. _____ 6. _____ 7. _____ 8. _____

9. _____ 10. _____ 11. _____ 12. _____

13. _____ 14. _____ 15. _____ 16. _____

Spelling patterns for u

ue	u • e	ui	ue

Read

true	dude	cube	fruit
blue	dune	cute	suit
due	flume	fume	juice
flue	prune	fuse	
	plume	huge	
	rule	mule	
	tube	mute	
	tune	use	

Write

1. _____   7. _____

2. _____   8. _____

3. _____   9. _____

4. _____   10. _____

5. _____   11. _____

6. _____   12. _____

Troublemakers

buy   building

u    U

Compare two sounds of u

us	cub	ruin	rube
cut	duck	tube	use
mull	jut	mule	cube
but	run	duke	butte
tub	rub	cute	jute

Write

1. _____   7. _____

2. _____   8. _____

3. _____   9. _____

4. _____   10. _____

5. _____   11. _____

6. _____   12. _____

Read

Cut the cube of butter.   The students understand.

Use the umbrella.   The fruit juice is for Sue.

Hug the duck.

a

1. _____

2. _____

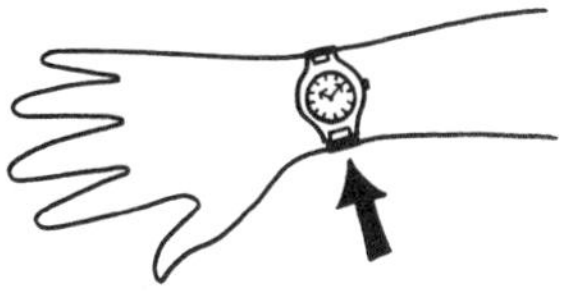

3. _____

4. _____

5. _____

6. _____

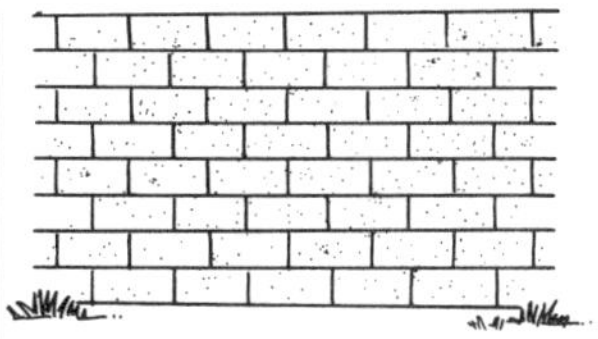

7. _____

8. _____

9. _____

10. _____

11. _____

12. _____

13. _____

14. _____

15. _____

16. _____

Spelling patterns for a

a

al   **wa**   **ar**

Read

al	wa	ar
all	wall	bar
fall	water	far
call	want	cart
ball	watch	market
tall	wash	park
talk	wad	star
walk	watt	hard

Write

1. _____   7. _____

2. _____   8. _____

3. _____   9. _____

4. _____   10. _____

5. _____   11. _____

6. _____   12. _____

Troublemakers

shall   valley

pal   gallon

calendar

Sounds Easy!©2002 Alta Book Center Publishers, San Francisco, California
Permission granted to photocopy for one teacher's classroom use only.

Compare two sounds of a

as	fad	fall	tar
tap	ran	water	start
can	happy	car	wash
map	tab	watch	tall
sat	has	salt	wall

Write

1. _____   7. _____

2. _____   8. _____

3. _____   9. _____

4. _____   10. _____

5. _____   11. _____

6. _____   12. _____

Read

Jan is always happy.   Start the car.
It's all salt water.   Watch the tall man.
Carl sat on the map!

Review   a

Compare

am	all	ate	ail
water	gas	game	Gail
bad	hall	father	shall
have	gave	want	paid
paid	hail	bait	ant

Write

1. _____   7. _____

2. _____   8. _____

3. _____   9. _____

4. _____   10. _____

5. _____   11. _____

6. _____   12. _____

Sounds Easy!©2002 Alta Book Center Publishers, San Francisco, California
Permission granted to photocopy for one teacher's classroom use only.

Read

Ann has a table.   The water is bad.
Father pays for the gas.   Has Jane come back?
Hail a taxi.   Can the baby play?

   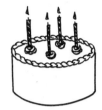

Compare

bike	gripe	grape	glade
file	lime	lake	main
glide	mine	fail	race
like	rice	tame	bait
time	bite	bake	lame

Write

1. _____

2. _____

3. _____

4. _____

5. _____

6. _____

7. _____

8. _____

9. _____

10. _____

11. _____

12. _____

Read

I like grapes.

David likes lime-ade.

The bike is mine.

Bake a cake.

Nina takes pie.

Sounds Easy!©2002 Alta Book Center Publishers, San Francisco, California
Permission granted to photocopy for one teacher's classroom use only.

Compare

add	hid	kick	aid
case	past	tape	hide
did	mice	dad	mace
bit	dime	bite	bait
wife	save	dame	had

Write

1. _____

2. _____

3. _____

4. _____

5. _____

6. _____

7. _____

8. _____

9. _____

10. _____

11. _____

12. _____

Read

Kick the tire.

Hide the dime.

Jack kisses his wife.

Tape the paper.

Time has passed.

Dad drank the wine.

a   o

 1. sacks

 2. socks

 3. map

 4. mop

 5. black

 6. block

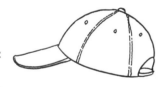 7. cap

 8. cop

 9. hat

 10. hot

Compare

an	hag	ox	bog
ax	tap	hog	cop
bag	tag	tog	pod
sack	pad	sock	top
cap	cab	on	cob

Write

1. _____   7. _____

2. _____   8. _____

3. _____   9. _____

4. _____   10. _____

5. _____   11. _____

6. _____   12. _____

Read

That hog is fat.   The tag is on the box.
Don's cap is black.   The cat ran to Tom.
The sock is in the bag.

1. ship

2. sheep

3. chick

4. cheek

5. hill

6. heel

7. fist

8. feast

9. slip

10. sleep

11. bit

12. beet

i    e

Compare

bid	pill	lead	feet
bin	ship	deep	bead
did	sit	bean	seat
dip	hip	deed	sheep
fit	lid	heap	peel

Write

1. _____   7. _____
2. _____   8. _____
3. _____   9. _____
4. _____   10. _____
5. _____   11. _____
6. _____   12. _____

Read

Six sheep eat weeds.   Sit on this seat.
Did it fit?   His feet are in the sink!
Eat these beans, please!

a   e

 1. pan

 2. pen

 3. ladder

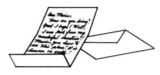 4. letter

 5. man

 6. men

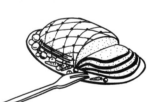 7. ham

 8. hem

 9. bat

 10. bet

Compare

bad	man	peck	hem
bag	pat	gem	led
ham	tan	beg	pet
jam	sat	set	bed
lad	pack	men	ten

Write

1. _____
2. _____
3. _____
4. _____
5. _____
6. _____

7. _____
8. _____
9. _____
10. _____
11. _____
12. _____

Read

Helen has her hat.
Get the jam.
Pet the hens.

Ten happy men sat in the taxi!
Pat went to bed.

Sounds Easy!©2002 Alta Book Center Publishers, San Francisco, California
Permission granted to photocopy for one teacher's classroom use only.

a   u

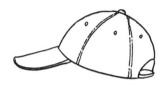 1. cap

 2. cup

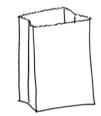 3. bag

 4. bug

 5. hat

 6. hut

 7. cat

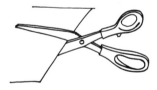 8. cut

 9. cab

 10. cub

a    **u**

Compare

hag	tag	bud	luck
as	cab	cub	mud
lack	bad	fun	rug
mad	fan	gull	tub
rag	gal	hug	us

Write

1. _____   7. _____

2. _____   8. _____

3. _____   9. _____

4. _____   10. _____

5. _____   11. _____

6. _____   12. _____

Read

Hug that cat.
Run to the taxi fast!

Dan is a lucky man.
What is that under the rug?

u   o

1. hug

2. hog

3. cup

4. cop

5. run

6. Ron

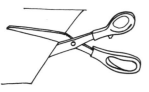
7. cut

8. cot

9. hut

10. hot

u    **o**

Compare

bug	jug	cod	lock
bucks	mum	boss	box
bus	nut	bog	jog
luck	sub	sob	not
hut	cud	hot	mom

Write

1. _____   7. _____

2. _____   8. _____

3. _____   9. _____

4. _____   10. _____

5. _____   11. _____

6. _____   12. _____

Read

Lock the box.   Jog around the block.

Bud's boss is upstairs.   My umbrella is on the bus!

Review

Compare

post	bad	wave	chose
shape	mop	hit	pod
lick	bite	pass	wise
paste	bid	chase	wife
ship	mope	hate	pad

Write

1. _____
2. _____
3. _____
4. _____
5. _____
6. _____

7. _____
8. _____
9. _____
10. _____
11. _____
12. _____

Read

Lick the stamp.

Mail the letter.

Mop the kitchen.

Bite the apple.

Fix the bike.

Review

Compare

odd	tape	kit	led
rag	pose	nine	fell
ox	dive	be	pat
add	kite	lad	dove
lid	rig	fail	Kate

Write

1. _____

2. _____

3. _____

4. _____

5. _____

6. _____

7. _____

8. _____

9. _____

10. _____

11. _____

12. _____

Read

Be happy!

Kate fell on the step.

Add the milk.

Stop the tape.

He feels lazy.

Review

Compare

zone	wag	chin	we
music	duck	gaze	nest
Tom	shine	Dick	wig
back	game	mile	mail
woke	sheep	wake	ship

Write

1. _____
2. _____
3. _____
4. _____
5. _____
6. _____

7. _____
8. _____
9. _____
10. _____
11. _____
12. _____

Read

Listen to the music.
He woke the baby.
Shine the windows.

Walk a mile.
Send the package.

Review

Compare

race	cat	hide	sit
hope	top	me	let
cute	luck	rice	hid
sight	lit	cut	lack
lick	let	rose	hop

Write

1. _____

2. _____

3. _____

4. _____

5. _____

6. _____

7. _____

8. _____

9. _____

10. _____

11. _____

12. _____

Sounds Easy!©2002 Alta Book Center Publishers, San Francisco, California
Permission granted to photocopy for one teacher's classroom use only.

Read

The sailboats are racing.

What a cute cat!

Cut the meat for the soup.

A rose is in the vase.

Eat the rice.

He plays hide and seek.

Review

Compare

sell	him	job	take
win	pipe	buzz	home
scene	bath	seal	hem
tick	wine	pit	boss
bass	pup	jam	Jim

Write

1. _____
2. _____
3. _____
4. _____
5. _____
6. _____

7. _____
8. _____
9. _____
10. _____
11. _____
12. _____

Read

She sells flowers.
Catch that fish!
Let's go home.

Jim likes Susan.
Bees buzz.

Section Three:
Initial
Clusters

(Photocopiable Exercises)

Name it!

(bl)

1. bl _____	2. bl _____	3. bl _____	4. bl _____
	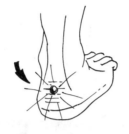		
5. bl _____	6. bl _____	7. bl _____	8. bl _____

Read • Add b

lack	___ lack
leach	___ leach
lend	___ lend
less	___ less
link	___ link
limp	___ limp
lock	___ lock
loom	___ loom
low	___ low

Listen • Write • Read

1. Is that your _____ dog?

2. A _____ is a kind of airplane.

3. My house is one _____ from here.

4. Don't _____ the whistle!

5. Flowers _____ in April.

6. Her hair is _____.

7. My new shoes give me _____.

8. The _____ is broken on my knife.

Name it!

(br)

1. br _____	2. br _____	3. br _____	4. br _____

4. br _____	6. br _____	7. br _____	8. br _____

Read • Add _b_

rake	___ rake
rag	___ rag
ran	___ ran
rain	___ rain
rave	___ rave
right	___ right
ring	___ ring
room	___ room

Listen • Write • Read

1. A _____ woman is not afraid.

2. The sun is very _____ today.

3. Use the _____ to clean the floor.

4. Do you have a comb and _____?

5. A _____ is part of a tree.

6. Some girls _____ their hair.

7. He has a gold _____.

8. _____ and cheese make a good

   sandwich.

(bl) (br)

Read	Add **l**	Add **r**
bed	b ___ ed	b ___ ed
bead	b ___ eed	b ___ eed
boom	b ___ oom	b ___ oom
bade	b ___ ade	b ___ aid

Listen • Write _bl_ or _br_

1. ___ anch   5. ___ oom   9. ___ ed

2. ___ ush   6. ___ anch   10. ___ oom

3. ___ ue   7. ___ ew   11. ___ ade

4. ___ ed   8. ___ ush   12. ___ aid

Listen • Write _bl_ or _br_

1. A ___ idge is over that river.

2. Where is my hair ___ ush?

3. She likes to ___ aid her hair.

4. Is he a ___ onde or a ___ unette?

5. The ___ anch is ___ oken off the tree.

6. Is this your ___ ue ___ anket?

Name it! (pl)

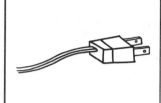			
1. pl _____	2. pl _____	3. pl _____	4. pl _____

5. pl _____	6. pl _____	7. pl _____	8. pl _____

Read • Add _p_

lay	___ lay
lane	___ lane
lug	___ lug
late	___ late
lank	___ lank
lump	___ lump
lace	___ lace
lease	___ lease

Listen • Write • Read

1. Can you _____ cards?

2. The old _____ is broken.

3. She's not very fat. She's _____.

4. Say " _____ " and "thank you".

5. They _____ peas in the garden.

6. She is wearing a _____ skirt.

7. A _____ is in the sky.

8. Please put the _____ in the sink.

Name it!   (pr)

1. pr _____	2. pr _____	3. pr _____	4. pr _____
	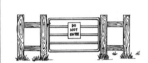		
5. pr _____	6. pr _____	7. pr _____	8. pr _____

Read • Add _p_

raise	___ raise
ray	___ ray
resident	___ resident
rice	___ rice
ride	___ ride
roof	___ roof

Listen • Write • Read

1. Thank you for the birthday _____.

2. That is a _____ office.

3. The son of the king is the _____.

4. If you rob a bank, you go to _____.

5. Don't write your name.

   Please _____ it.

6. I go to church to _____.

7. What does it cost? What is the

   _____?

8. His dog is going to win first _____.

Sounds Easy!©2002 Alta Book Center Publishers, San Francisco, California
Permission granted to photocopy for one teacher's classroom use only.

(pl) (pr)

Read	Add **l**	Add **r**
pay	p ___ ay	p ___ ay
pie	p ___ y	p ___ y
peasant	p ___ easant	p ___ esent

Listen • Write _pl_ or _pr_

1. ___ ank
2. ___ ow
3. ___ ay
4. ___ easant

5. ___ um
6. ___ ank
7. ___ esent
8. ___ astic

9. ___ oblem
10. ___ ow
11. ___ actice
12. ___ aise

Listen • Write _pl_ or _pr_

1. ___ unes and ___ ums are fruits.

2. He's not going to ___ ay baseball.

3. I need to ___ actice my English!

4. The dishes are made of ___ astic.

5. A farmer has a ___ ow to make a garden.

6. ___ ease sit down.

Review Vocabulary

(bl) (br) (pl) (pr)

1. ___ acelet	2. ___ ize	3. ___ ade	4. ___ ug
5. ___ ister	6. ___ ant	7. ___ ince	8. ___ aid
9. ___ ice	10. ___ anch	11. ___ oom	12. ___ ison
13. ___ idge	14. ___ aid	15. ___ int	16. ___ ood

Printing Printing

Name it! (cl)

1. cl _____	2. cl _____	3. cl _____	4. cl _____

5. cl _____	6. cl _____	7. cl _____	8. cl _____

Read • Add c

lamp	___ lamp
lay	___ lay
lean	___ lean
left	___ left
lever	___ lever
log	___ log
lock	___ lock
lap	___ lap
lash	___ lash

Listen • Write • Read

1. I wash my _____ on Saturday.

2. Your shoes are in the _____.

3. A small plant with three leaves is a

   _____.

4. Don't stand next to the _____!

5. What time is it? Look at the _____.

6. The cat likes to _____ a tree.

7. Put a _____ on your papers.

8. A _____ is a tool for fixing things.

Name it! (cr)

1. cr _____	2. cr _____	3. cr _____	4. cr _____

5. cr _____	6. cr _____	7. cr _____	8. cr _____

Read • Add _c_

rack	___ rack
rash	___ rash
raft	___ raft
rib	___ rib
rock	___ rock
rook	___ rook
row	___ row

Listen • Write • Read

1. It's okay to _____ when you're sad.

2. A king's hat is a _____.

3. Children write with _____.

4. A _____ lives in the ocean.

5. An insect that sings at night is a

   _____.

6. A bed for a baby is a _____.

7. The police are looking for the

   _____.

8. If you need help, call the Red

   _____.

Sounds Easy!©2002 Alta Book Center Publishers, San Francisco, California. Permission granted to photocopy for one teacher's classroom use only.

(cl) (cr)

Read	**Add l**	**Add r**
camp	c ___ amp	c ___ amp
cash	c ___ ash	c ___ ash
cock	c ___ ock	c ___ ock
Coke	c ___ oak	c ___ oak

Listen • Write cl or cr

1. ___ ack	5. ___ ash	9. ___ owds
2. ___ aw	6. ___ ack	10. ___ ash
3. ___ ass	7. ___ ouds	11. ___ aw
4. ___ ock	8. ___ ass	12. ___ ock

Listen • Write cl or cr

1. We like our English ___ ass.

2. Many people in one place is a ___ owd.

3. You see ___ ouds in the sky when it rains.

4. Finger nails on a cat are ___ aws.

5. A car accident is a ___ ash.

6. A tool for holding two things together is a ___ amp.

Name it! (gl)

1. gl _____	2. gl _____	3. gl _____	4. gl _____

Read • Add _g_

lad   ___ lad

lance   ___ lance

lass   ___ lass

laze   ___ laze

lade   ___ lade

litter   ___ litter

lobe   ___ lobe

loom   ___ loom

loss   ___ loss

love   ___ love

Listen • Write • Read

1. When it is cold, we wear _____.

2. Another word for "happy" is _____.

3. Don't break the _____ please.

4. A _____ is a map of the world.

5. A quick look is a _____.

6. Shiny paint is _____.

7. We use _____ to fix broken things.

8. Sometimes donuts have a sugar

     _____.

Name it! (gr)

1. gr _____

2. gr _____

3. gr _____

4. g _____

5. gr _____

6. gr _____

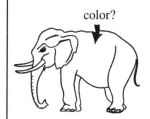

color?

7. gr _____

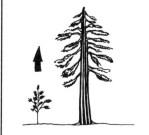

8. gr _____

Read • Add _g_

rain	___ rain
rave	___ rave
ray	___ ray
raze	___ raze
room	___ room
round	___ round
row	___ row

Listen • Write • Read

1. A _____ is a big smile.

2. Cows and horses eat _____.

3. Bread is made from _____.

4. The _____ brushed the dog.

5. _____ are small purple fruit.

6. Water and sun make flowers _____.

7. My father's mother is my _____.

8. The color of elephants is _____.

Read	Add __l__	Add __r__
gas	g ___ ass	g ___ ass
gaze	g ___ aze	g ___ aze
go	g ___ ow	g ___ ow
goo	g ___ ue	g ___ ew

Listen • Write _gl_ or _gr_

1. ___ ass	5. ___ aze	9. ___ oss
2. ___ oom	6. ___ ade	10. ___ ew
3. ___ ue	7. ___ oom	11. ___ ass
4. ___ eam	8. ___ een	12. ___ aze

Listen • Write _gl_ or _gr_

1. Our children ___ ow quickly.

2. Please give me the bottle of ___ ue.

3. The ___ ass is very ___ een in the park.

4. The lamp is made of ___ ass.

5. Cook the steak on the ___ ill.

6. The teacher gave me a good ___ ade on my homework.

Review Vocabulary

1. ___ ue

2. ___ y

3. ___ icket

4. ___ amp

5. ___ over

6. ___ own

7. ___ andma

8. ___ obe

9. ___ ass

10. ___ oset

11. ___ oss

12. ___ ain

13. ___ ayon

14. ___ ass

15. ___ in

16. ___ iff

Review Vocabulary   (bl) (br) (pl) (pr) (cl) (cr) (gl) (gr)

Listen • Write

1. ___ oom
2. ___ ack
3. ___ ay
4. ___ int
5. ___ own
6. ___ an
7. ___ ush
8. ___ eed

9. ___ ush
10. ___ oom
11. ___ ay
12. ___ an
13. ___ ush
14. ___ int
15. ___ oom
16. ___ ack

17. ___ own
18. ___ ack
19. ___ ate
20. ___ eed
21. ___ own
22. ___ oom
23. ___ ush
24. ___ ay

Name it!

1. _____

2. _____

3. _____

4. _____

5. _____

6. _____

7. _____

8. _____

Name it! (fl)

	 	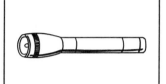	
1. fl_____	2. fl_____	3. fl_____	4. fl_____

5. fl_____	6. fl_____	7. fl_____	8. fl_____

Read • Add f

lag	___ lag
lake	___ lake
lame	___ lame
light	___ light
lock	___ lock
lush	___ lush
lunk	___ lunk

Listen • Write • Read

1. The American _____ is red, white and blue.

2. The fire on a candle is a _____.

3. A light you carry when camping is a _____.

4. An insect that likes dogs is a _____.

5. Roses and daisies are _____.

6. A small piece of snow is a _____.

7. A _____ is a musical instrument.

8. Many sheep together is a _____.

Name it! (fr)

1. fr _____	2. fr _____	3. fr _____	4. fr _____ _____

5. Fr _____	6. fr _____	7. fr _____	8. fr _____

Read • Add r

fame	f ___ ame
fee	f ___ ee
fend	f ___ iend
fog	f ___ og
fight	f ___ ight

Listen • Write • Read

1. We cook eggs in a _____ _____.

2. The students are good _____.

3. He has _____ on his nose.

4. Mr. DuFils is from _____.

5. Bananas and apples are _____.

6. A little green animal is a _____.

7. If it has no price, it is _____.

8. Around the picture is a _____.

(fl) (fr)

Read	Add **l**	Add **r**
fame	f ___ ame	f ___ ame
fee	f ___ ee	f ___ ee
fight	f ___ ight	f ___ ight
food	f ___ ute	f ___ uit

Listen • Write **fl** or **fr**

1. ___ esh
2. ___ ank
3. ___ ight
4. ___ uit

5. ___ ame
6. ___ ight
7. ___ esh
8. ___ eezer

9. ___ ank
10. ___ ute
11. ___ eight
12. ___ ont

Listen • Write **fl** or **fr**

1. Is this fish ___ esh?

2. What kind of ___ uit do you like?

3. Put the ice cream in the ___ eezer.

4. Can she play the ___ ute?

5. Don't sit in back. Sit in ___ ont.

6. The tickets are ___ ee!

Name it!   (tr)

1. tr _____	2. tr _____	3. tr _____	4. tr _____

5. tr _____	6. tr _____	7. tr _____	8. tr _____

Read • Add t

rain	___ rain
ray	___ ray
rap	___ rap
read	___ read
rip	___ rip

Listen • Write • Read

1. A pine is a kind of _____.

2. A pick-up is a kind of _____.

3. A _____ is slower than an airplane.

4. Serve the lunch on a _____.

5. The mouse is in the _____.

6. Put the blankets in the _____.

7. _____ and guitars are musical instruments.

8. In the mountains we walk on a _____.

Sounds Easy! ©2002 Alta Book Center Publishers, San Francisco, California. Permission granted to photocopy for one teacher's classroom use only.

Name it! (dr)

1. dr _____

2. dr _____

3. dr _____

4. dr _____

5. dr _____

6. dr _____

7. dr _____

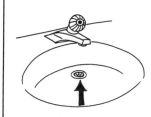

8. dr _____

Read • Add d

rain   ___ rain

rum   ___ rum

rink   ___ rink

rag   ___ rag

raw   ___ raw

rift   ___ rift

rip   ___ rip

rugs   ___ rugs

Listen • Write • Read

1. A woman wears a _____.

2. Coffee is a hot _____.

3. A _____ is a musical instrument.

4. I _____ when I sleep.

5. Penicillin is a _____.

6. Can you _____ a car?

7. _____ are long curtains.

8. Water in the sink goes down the _____.

Read	**Add _d_**	**Add _t_**
rain	___ rain	___ rain
rill	___ rill	___ rill
red	___ read	___ read

Listen • Write _dr_ or _tr_

1. ___ ail	5. ___ ess	9. ___ ip
2. ___ uck	6. ___ ue	10. ___ ip
3. ___ y	7. ___ y	11. ___ ink
4. ___ ee	8. ___ op	12. ___ apes

Listen • Write _dr_ or _tr_

1. An apple ___ ee is in front of my house.

2. Can you ___ ive a ___ uck?

3. I'm taking a ___ ain to Los Angeles.

4. ___ y your hands on the towel.

5. She's wearing a new red ___ ess.

6. Please ___ aw me a picture of a horse.

Review Vocabulary

1. ___ uit

2. ___ unk

3. ___ ance

4. ___ ap

5. ___ ee

6. ___ ood

7. ___ ail

8. ___ iends

9. ___ umpet

10. ___ ee

11. ___ eckles

12. ___ ea

13. ___ ashlight

14. ___ eam

15. ___ uck

16. ___ ugs

Name it! (th) (thr)

1. th _____	2. th _____	3. th _____ _____	4. th _____
3			
5. th _____	6. th _____	7. th _____	8. th _____

Listen • Write • Read

1. If you want to sew on a button you need _____.

2. He's not fat. He's _____.

3. Susan has _____ sisters.

4. Do you _____ about your family?

5. I want to say "_____ you" for the present

6. _____ the ball to me!

7. I have a cold. My _____ is sore.

8. The _____ took the money from the bank.

Sounds Easy!©2002 Alta Book Center Publishers, San Francisco, California
Permission granted to photocopy for one teacher's classroom use only.

Review Vocabulary

Listen • Write

1. ___ ain
2. ___ iends
3. ___ ame
4. ___ um
5. ___ in
6. ___ uck
7. ___ og
8. ___ ead

9. ___ ue
10. ___ aw
11. ___ ink
12. ___ uit
13. ___ uck
14. ___ ute
15. ___ ink
16. ___ oat

17. ___ ee
18. ___ ag
19. ___ ay
20. ___ ame
21. ___ esser
22. ___ ip
23. ___ y
24. ___ ief

Name it!

1. tr _____

2. fl _____

3. dr _____

4. fr _____

5. th _____

6. thr _____

7. fl _____

8. fr _____

Review Vocabulary

(fl) (fr) (tr) (dr) (th) (thr)

1. ___ ivate	2. ___ ate	3. ___ onde	4. ___ othes
5. ___ ay	6. ___ ay	7. ___ ying pan	8. ___ ab
9. ___ ive	10. ___ ind	11. ___ ay	12. ___ um
13. ___ oom	14. ___ ip	15. ___ ain	16. ___ ook

color?

Name it!

(sp) (spr) (spl)

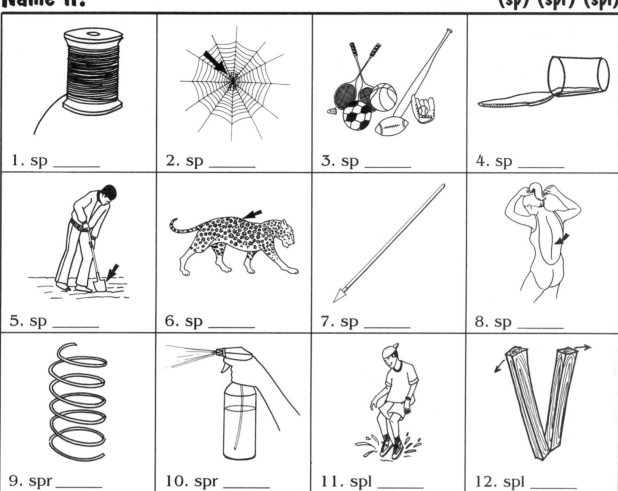

1. sp _____

2. sp _____

3. sp _____

4. sp _____

5. sp _____

6. sp _____

7. sp _____

8. sp _____

9. spr _____

10. spr _____

11. spl _____

12. spl _____

Read • Add sp

ray	___ ray
ring	___ ring
rocket	___ rocket
lash	___ lash
lit	___ lit
latter	___ latter
end	___ end
it	___ it
oil	___ oil

Listen • Write • Read

1. I need a _____ of black thread.

2. Baseball and tennis are _____.

3. I'm afraid of _____.

4. Please don't _____ the milk.

5. _____ the garden with the hose.

6. Babies like to _____ in the bath.

7. A leopard has _____.

8. I always _____ too much money at the market.

Name it!

(st) (str)

 1. st _____	 2. st _____	 3. st _____	 4. st _____
 5. st _____	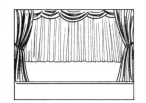 6. st _____	 7. st _____	 8. str _____
 9. str _____	 10. str _____	 11. str _____	 12. str _____

Read

seam	steam	stream
sand	stand	strand
sing	sting	string

Listen • Write • Read

1. Do you have a postage _____.

2. A _____ is a small river.

3. I ate too much. My _____ hurts.

4. The _____ on my kite is broken.

5. The _____ are beautiful tonight.

6. Hot water makes _____.

7. Are you a new _____?

8. Musicians _____ on a

_____.

Sounds Easy!©2002 Alta Book Center Publishers, San Francisco, California
Permission granted to photocopy for one teacher's classroom use only.

Name it!

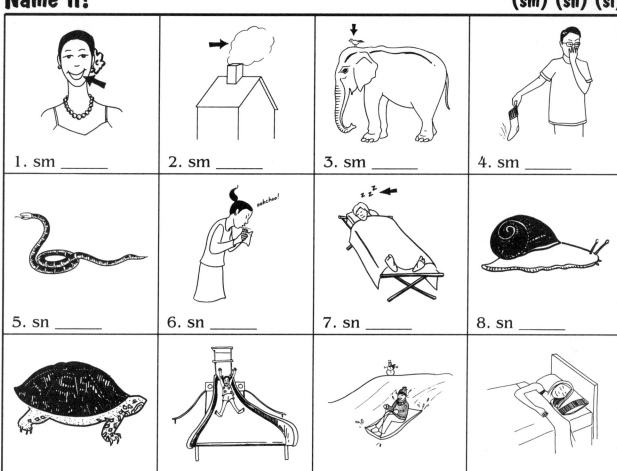

1. sm _____

2. sm _____

3. sm _____

4. sm _____

5. sn _____

6. sn _____

7. sn _____

8. sn _____

9. sl _____

10. sl _____

11. sl _____

12. sl _____

Read • Add s

mash	___ mash
mile	___ mile
mall	___ mall
lap	___ lap
lender	___ lender
low	___ low
nap	___ nap
nail	___ nail

Listen • Write • Read

1. Do you _____ _____?

2. A _____ is very _____.

3. Does your husband _____?

4. Don't be sad. _____!

5. Is that your _____ dog?

6. Children like to play on a _____.

7. That _____ was three feet long!

8. When you have a cold, you _____.

Review Vocabulary

(s + consonant)

Read

spring	speak	spay	spy	splash
sting	streak	stray	sty	stash
string	sneak	spray	spry	smash
sling	sleek	stay	sly	slash

Listen • Write • Read

1. Do you _____ eak Chinese?

2. She doesn't buy hair _____ ay.

3. A bee _____ ing hurts!

4. I want four _____ all tomatoes, please.

5. I need some _____ ing for my kite.

6. He's wearing a _____ aw hat.

7. Does it _____ ow in Egypt?

8. Take a taxi. The bus is too _____ ow.

9. Where are you going to _____ ay?

10. Look out! There's a _____ ake!

Review Vocabulary

(s + consonant)

1. _____ ool

2. _____ all

3. _____ amp

4. _____ aw

5. _____ ike

6. _____ ing

7. _____ ore

8. _____ orts

9. _____ ing

10. _____ ash

11. _____ ow

12. _____ oke

13. _____ ake

14. _____ eeze

15. _____ ove

16. _____ ay

Name it!

(sc) (scr) (sq) (sk)

1. sq _____   2. sq _____   3. sq _____   4. sq _____

5. sc _____   6. sc _____   7. sc _____   8. sk _____

9. sk _____   10. sk _____   11. scr _____   12. scr _____

Read • Add _s_

Kate	___ kate
key	___ ki
kin	___ kin
car	___ car
cool	___ chool
care	___ care
cream	___ cream

Listen • Write • Read

1. Can you ice _____?

2. A _____ has four sides.

3. _____ the lemons to make lemonade.

4. Fix the table with a _____.

5. Do you have a short _____?

6. My _____ keeps my neck warm.

7. Do you like to water _____?

8. Dogs always _____ their fleas.

Review Vocabulary

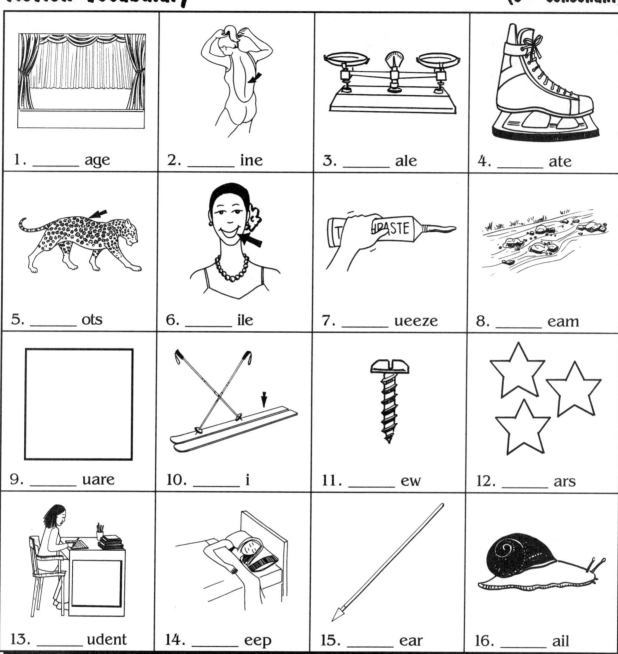

1. _____ age

2. _____ ine

3. _____ ale

4. _____ ate

5. _____ ots

6. _____ ile

7. _____ ueeze

8. _____ eam

9. _____ uare

10. _____ i

11. _____ ew

12. _____ ars

13. _____ udent

14. _____ eep

15. _____ ear

16. _____ ail

Name it!

(sh) (shr)

1. sh _____	2. sh _____	3. sh _____	4. sh _____
	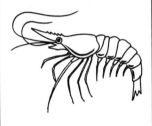	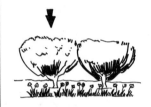	
5. sh _____	6. shr _____	7. shr _____	8. shr _____

Read • Add h

sake	s ___ ake
save	s ___ ave
see	s ___ e
sell	s ___ ell
sip	s ___ ip
sock	s ___ ock
sore	s ___ ore
sow	s ___ ow

Read • Add hr

sink	s ___ ink
sign	s ___ ine
sub	s ___ ub
said	s ___ ed

Listen • Write • Read

1. Where is my other _____?
2. Are my white _____ dirty?
3. The party is in one hour. You have to _____ and _____!
4. Cotton _____ _____ sometimes in the washing machine.
5. Let's go to the _____.
6. Plant the _____ next to the house.
7. A _____ is a farm animal.
8. This _____ will go to Japan.

Review Vocabulary

1. _____

2. _____

3. _____

4. _____

5. _____

6. _____

7. _____

8. _____

9. _____

10. _____

11. _____

12. _____

13. _____

14. _____

15. _____

16. _____

Review Vocabulary

1. _____

2. _____

3. _____

4. _____

5. _____

6. _____

7. _____

8. _____

9. _____

10. _____

11. _____

12. _____

13. _____

14. _____

15. _____

16. _____

Review Vocabulary

1. _____

2. _____

3. _____

4. _____

5. _____

6. _____

7. _____

8. _____

9. _____

10. _____

11. _____

12. _____

13. _____

14. _____

15. _____

16. _____

Review Vocabulary

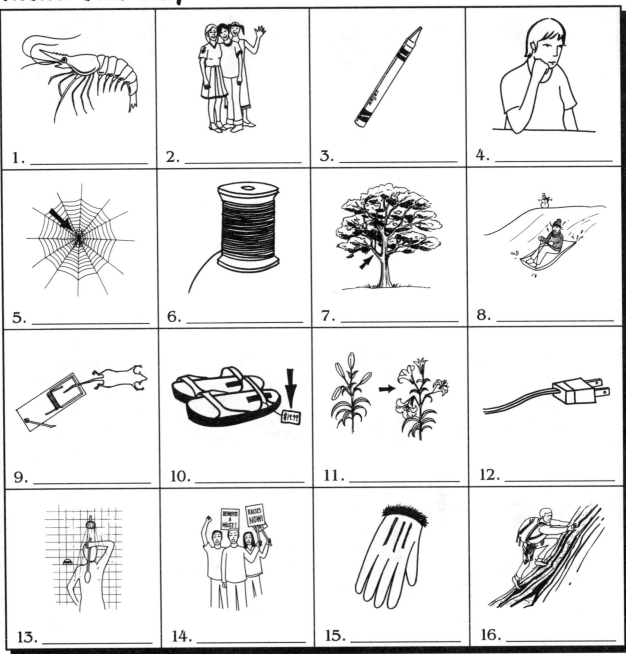

1. _____

2. _____

3. _____

4. _____

5. _____

6. _____

7. _____

8. _____

9. _____

10. _____

11. _____

12. _____

13. _____

14. _____

15. _____

16. _____

Review Vocabulary

1. _____

2. _____

3. _____

4. _____

5. _____

6. _____

7. _____

8. _____

9. _____

10. _____

11. _____

12. _____

13. _____

14. _____

15. _____

16. _____

Section Four:
Final
Clusters

(Photocopiable Exercises)

Name it!

Final b clusters

1. _____ b

2. _____ be

3. _____ b

4. _____ be

5. _____ b

6. _____ b

7. _____ bs

8. _____ be

Read	Add <u>s</u>	Add <u>bed</u>	Read	Add <u>d</u>
rob	rob ___	rob _____	robe	robe ___
fib	fib ___	fib _____	cube	cube ___
rub	rub ___	rub _____		
sob	sob ___	sob _____		
web	web ___	web _____		

Listen • Write • Read

1. Who _____ that bank yesterday?

2. _____ are baby bears.

3. The sugar _____ are on the table.

4. He _____ his tired feet.

5. Please buy three _____ of toothpaste.

6. Babies usually wear _____ when they eat.

Name it!

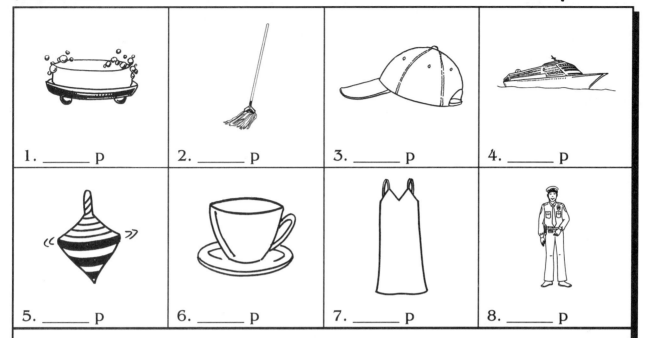

1. _____ p

2. _____ p

3. _____ p

4. _____ p

5. _____ p

6. _____ p

7. _____ p

8. _____ p

Read	Add _s_	Add _ped_
map	map ___	map _____
zip	zip ___	zip _____
slip	slip ___	slip _____
ship	ship ___	ship _____
soap	soap ___	**Add _d_**
tape	tape ___	tape ___
type	type ___	type ___

Listen • Write • Read

1. Where are our _____ of China?

2. She has three CDs and four _____.

3. Bill _____ his jacket and went out.

4. How many _____ of coffee did you drink?

5. Mr. Lewis _____ the floor yesterday.

6. The secretary _____ forty letters this morning!

Read

taps	mopped	laps
tabs	mobbed	labs
cups	roped	
cubs	robed	

Listen • Write __bbed__ __pped__ __ps__ __bs__

1. ro _____ 5. zi _____ 9. slee _____

2. fi _____ 6. soa _____ 10. ri _____

3. so _____ 7. kee _____ 11. mo _____

4. ma _____ 8. ru _____ 12. ri _____

Listen • Write • Read

1. The cowboy _____ the horse in the field.

2. _____ is another word for "steals."

3. _____ is another word for "cries."

4. When it was cold, she _____ her jacket.

5. Mother _____ her shoes under the bed.

6. He is so thin you can see his _____.

Sounds Easy!©2002 Alta Book Center Publishers, San Francisco, California
Permission granted to photocopy for one teacher's classroom use only.

Name it!

Final d and t clusters

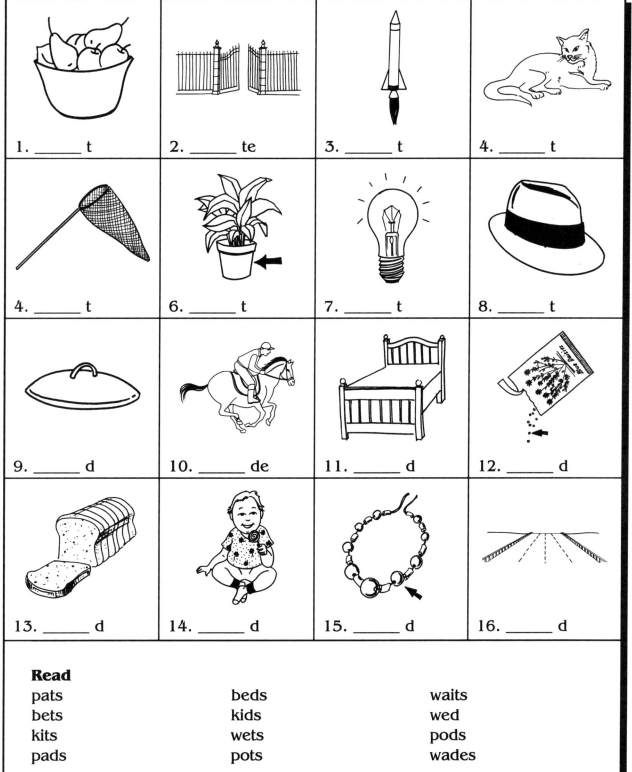

1. _____ t

2. _____ te

3. _____ t

4. _____ t

4. _____ t

6. _____ t

7. _____ t

8. _____ t

9. _____ d

10. _____ de

11. _____ d

12. _____ d

13. _____ d

14. _____ d

15. _____ d

16. _____ d

Read

pats	beds	waits
bets	kids	wed
kits	wets	pods
pads	pots	wades

Compare final b, p, d and t clusters

Listen • Write bs   ps   ts   ds

1. ca ___

2. ma ___

3. ste ___

4. ro ___

5. tu ___

6. sou ___

7. be ___

8. boo ___

9. ligh ___

10. ne ___

11. roa ___

12. bi ___

Listen • Write • Read

1. Use these _____ to clean, please.

2. The new _____ are on the table.

3. Where are your fishing _____?

4. What kind of _____ are on the menu?

5. She's not eating the red _____.

6. Please put on your _____ because it's muddy.

7. Susan and Marta are changing the _____.

Name it!

Final ch clusters

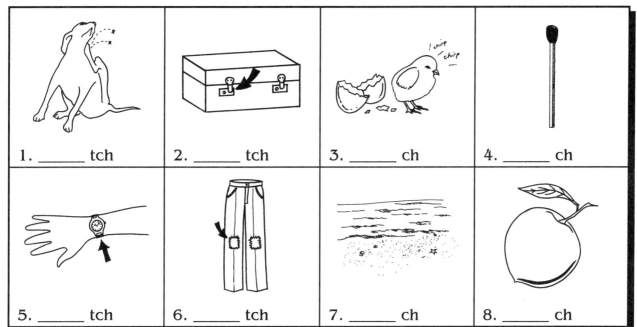

1. _____ tch	2. _____ tch	3. _____ ch	4. _____ ch
5. _____ tch	6. _____ tch	7. _____ ch	8. _____ ch

Read	**Add _ed_**
hatch	hatch ___
patch	patch ___
watch	watch ___
reach	reach ___
hitch	hitch ___
touch	touch ___
scratch	scratch ___

Listen • Write • Read

1. Mother _____ my old jeans.

2. Bob never _____ the snake.

3. Jack _____ the trailer to the car.

4. She _____ football on T.V. with her husband.

5. The baby ducks _____ on Thursday.

6. She _____ school at nine o'clock.

7. The dog _____ his flea bites.

Name it!

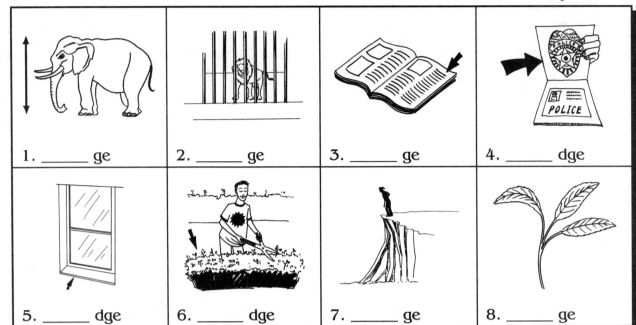

1. _____ ge

2. _____ ge

3. _____ ge

4. _____ dge

5. _____ dge

6. _____ dge

7. _____ ge

8. _____ ge

Read	Add **d**	Listen • Write • Read

Read

rage

cage

edge

lodge

Add d

rage ___

cage ___

edge ___

lodge ___

Listen • Write • Read

1. The bird was _____.

2. A policeman wears a _____.

3. Turn to _____ six in your book.

4. Don't stand too near the _____!

5. A special plant for cooking is _____.

6. Someone who is very angry is

   "in a _____."

7. Bushes planted close together are

   called a _____.

Name it!   Final sh clusters

1. _____ sh

2. _____ sh

3. _____ sh

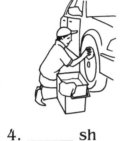

4. _____ sh

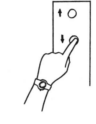

5. _____ sh

6. _____ sh

Read	**Add _ed_**
fish	fish ___
dish	dish ___
cash	cash ___
wash	wash ___
push	push ___
crash	crash ___

Listen • Write • Read

1. She _____ the check at the bank on Monday.

2. Jack _____ his clothes.

3. I think she _____ her car into a bus!

4. Last summer I _____ in Lake Tahoe.

5. She _____ the baby in the stroller.

6. Mother _____ up the dinner.

Compare final ch, g, and sh clusters

Listen • Write <u>tched</u> <u>ged</u> <u>shed</u>

1. wa _____

2. wa _____

3. pu _____

4. ca _____

5. ca _____

6. di _____

7. pa _____

8. cra _____

9. di _____

10. ra _____

11. ha _____

12. hed _____

Listen • Write • Read

1. Who _____ the T.V. this afternoon?

2. The bird is not _____.

3. The child _____ for the candy.

4. The chicks _____ yesterday.

5. She _____ her paycheck on Friday.

6. Are his old blue jeans _____?

7. The car didn't start, so the boys _____ it.

8. She _____ her new car.

Review Vocabulary

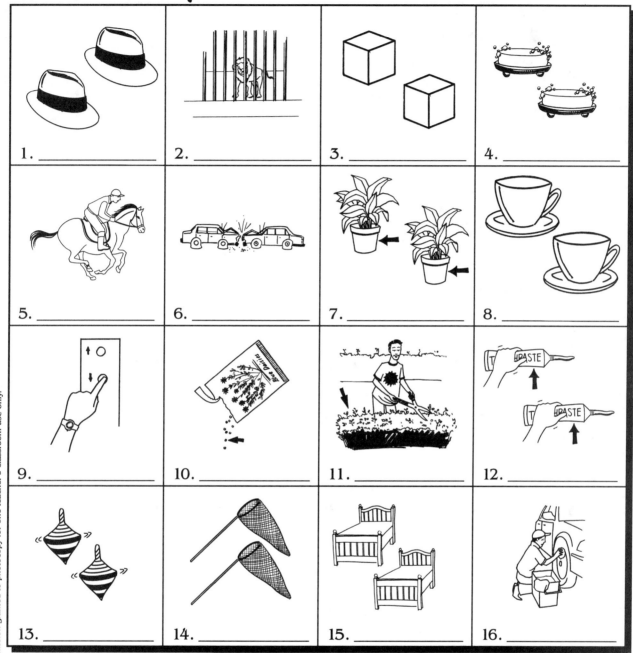

1. _____

2. _____

3. _____

4. _____

5. _____

6. _____

7. _____

8. _____

9. _____

10. _____

11. _____

12. _____

13. _____

14. _____

15. _____

16. _____

Name it!

1. _____ g
2. _____ g
3. _____ g
4. _____ g
5. _____ g
6. _____ g
7. _____ g
8. _____ g

Read	**Add s**	**Add ged**
bag	bag ___	bag _____
tag	tag ___	tag _____
sag	sag ___	sag _____
flag	flag ___	flag _____
beg	beg ___	beg _____
jog	jog ___	jog _____
hog	hog ___	hog _____

Listen • Write • Read

1. How many _____ are in our yard?

2. The _____ are flying today because it's a holiday.

3. My _____ are tired from standing.

4. The poor man _____ for money on the street.

5. They _____ my suitcase at the airport.

6. She _____ every day. It's good exercise.

Name it!

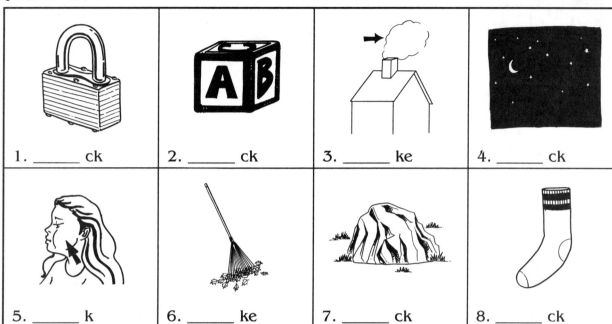

1. _____ ck
2. _____ ck
3. _____ ke
4. _____ ck
5. _____ k
6. _____ ke
7. _____ ck
8. _____ ck

Read	**Add s**	**Add ed**
back	back ___	back ____
lock	lock ___	lock ____
book	book ___	book ____
check	check ___	check ____
look	look ___	look ____
pick	pick ___	pick ____

Listen • Write • Read

1. The girls _____ flowers.

2. The _____ are green and yellow.

3. They _____ their homework.

4. Maria _____ beautiful in her red dress.

5. Grandpa _____ the yard.

6. They always _____ the door.

7. It's too bad that Henry _____.

8. Are these your _____?

Name it!   Final x clusters

1. _____ x

6

2. _____ x

3. _____ x

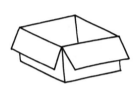

4. _____ x

5. _____ x

6. _____ x

Read	**Add _ed_**	**Read**
axe	ax ____	text
wax	wax ____	next
box	box ____	
mix	mix ____	
tax	tax ____	

Listen • Write • Read

1. Mother _____ the milk and eggs.

2. The clerk _____ the groceries.

3. Lucy _____ the car.

4. This English _____ book is easy!

5. _____ Monday we are not going to school.

6. Did you pay the _____?

7. She has _____ boyfriends!

Compare final g, k, and x clusters

Read

tags	tagged	tacks	tacked
pegs	pegged	pecks	pecked
bags	bagged	backs	backed

Listen • Write <u>gs</u> <u>gged</u> <u>cks</u> <u>cked</u>

1. ta _____   5. pe _____   9. ta _____

2. ba _____   6. ba _____   10. pe _____

3. pe _____   7. ta _____   11. ba _____

4. ta _____   8. ba _____   12. pe _____

Listen • Write • Read

1. The map is _____ to the wall.

2. The chickens _____ at the corn.

3. Are the price _____ on the shirts?

4. The thumb _____ are in the desk.

5. Will you please carry my _____?

6. The salesman _____ the clothes on sale.

7. _____ are small nails made of wood.

8. Uncle Peter _____ his car into the garage.

Name it!

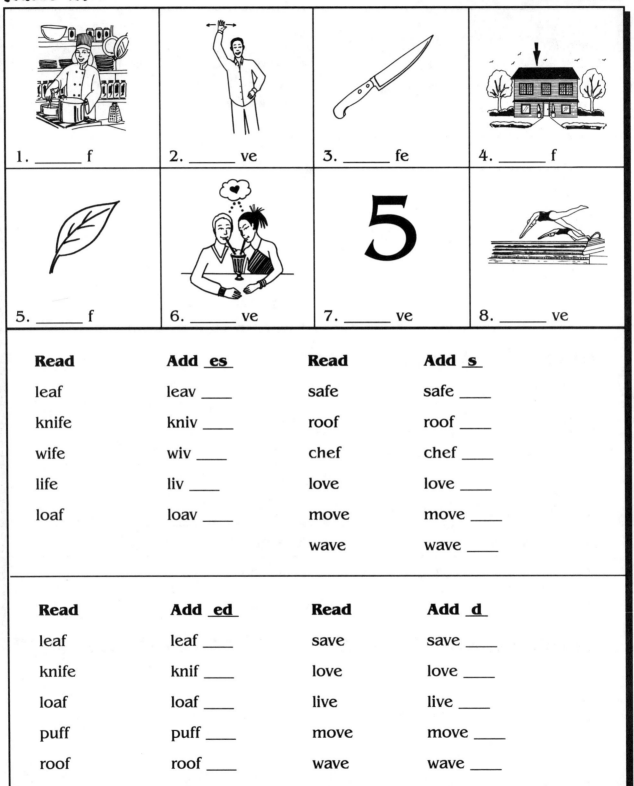

1. _____ f

2. _____ ve

3. _____ fe

4. _____ f

5. _____ f

6. _____ ve

7. _____ ve

8. _____ ve

Read	**Add es**	**Read**	**Add s**
leaf	leav ___	safe	safe ___
knife	kniv ___	roof	roof ___
wife	wiv ___	chef	chef ___
life	liv ___	love	love ___
loaf	loav ___	move	move ___
		wave	wave ___

Read	**Add ed**	**Read**	**Add d**
leaf	leaf ___	save	save ___
knife	knif ___	love	love ___
loaf	loaf ___	live	live ___
puff	puff ___	move	move ___
roof	roof ___	wave	wave ___

Sounds Easy!©2002 Alta Book Center Publishers, San Francisco, California. Permission granted to photocopy for one teacher's classroom use only.

Name it!

1. _____

2. _____

3. _____

4. _____

5. _____

5 5

6. _____

7. _____

8. _____

Listen • Write • Read

1. _____

2. _____

3. _____

4. _____

5. _____

6. _____

7. _____

8. _____

Name it!

Final ld and lt clusters

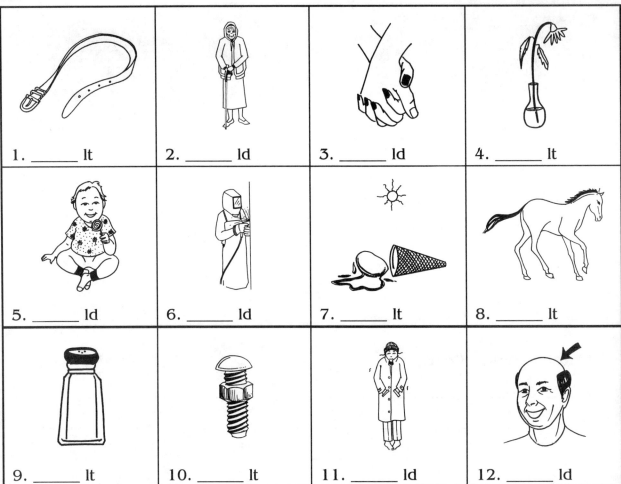

1. _____ lt   2. _____ ld   3. _____ ld   4. _____ lt

5. _____ ld   6. _____ ld   7. _____ lt   8. _____ lt

9. _____ lt   10. _____ lt   11. _____ ld   12. _____ ld

1. Please pass the _____.

2. She bought two _____.

3. The _____ sat on the floor and played.

4. The _____ man has many stories to tell.

5. The _____ are in a small box in the garage.

6. She _____ the baby's hand when he walks.

7. With no water, the flowers _____.

Name it!

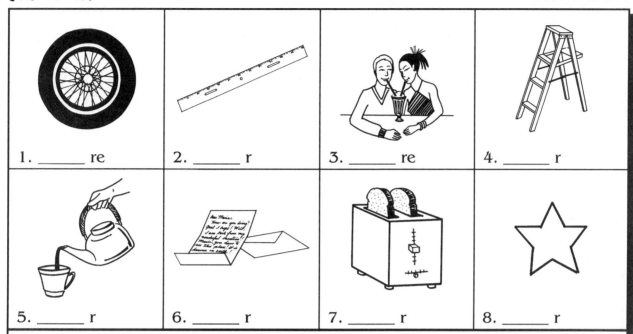

1. _____ re

2. _____ r

3. _____ re

4. _____ r

5. _____ r

6. _____ r

7. _____ r

8. _____ r

Read	Add **s**	Add **ed**
star	star ___	starr ___
pour	pour ___	pour ___
share	share ___	share ___

Listen • Write • Read

1. She wrote two _____ to her sisters.

2. He _____ the coffee into the cup.

3. We need new _____ on the car.

4. They looked at several _____ before they bought one.

5. The students had _____ in their desks.

6. The workers used _____ to pick the apples.

7. There are fifty _____ on the American flag.

8. The children _____ the cookies.

Name it!

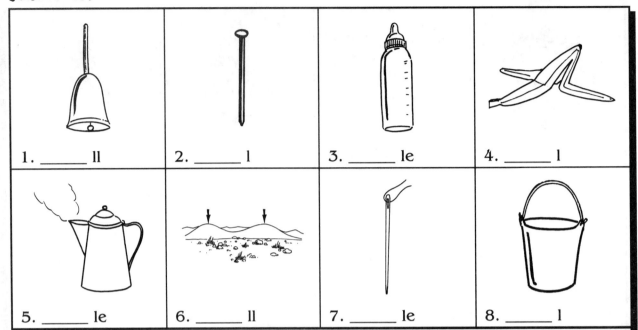

1. _____ ll

2. _____ l

3. _____ le

4. _____ l

5. _____ le

6. _____ ll

7. _____ le

8. _____ l

Read	Add _s_	Add _ed_
call	call ___	call ___
peel	peel ___	peel ___
nail	nail ___	nail ___
mail	mail ___	mail ___
roll	roll ___	roll ___

Listen • Write • Read

1. The _____ of California are beautiful.

2. She _____ the orange for her son.

3. The boys _____ the ball on the floor.

4. She _____ the letters in the mailbox on the corner.

5. He drank three full _____ of orange juice!

6. Where are the _____? I need to fix the table.

7. Grandmother _____ the doctor's office.

8. I can hear the church _____ from the home.

Compare final r and l clusters

Listen • Write <u>rs</u> <u>ls</u> <u>red</u> <u>led</u>

1. fi _____

2. fi _____

3. ca _____

4. pee _____

5. sta _____

6. fi _____

7. pee _____

8. pee _____

9. pee _____

Listen • Write • Read

1. She keeps her papers in the _____.

2. He _____ his mother last night.

3. The monkey _____ the banana.

4. She wrote her name on a _____.

5. Long distance phone _____ cost more money.

6. The business man _____ his reports in the cabinet.

7. There are too many _____ on this freeway!

Review Vocabulary

1. _____

2. _____

3. _____

4. _____

5. _____

6. _____

7. _____

8. _____

9. _____

10. _____

11. _____

12. _____

13. _____

14. _____

15. _____

16. _____

Name it!

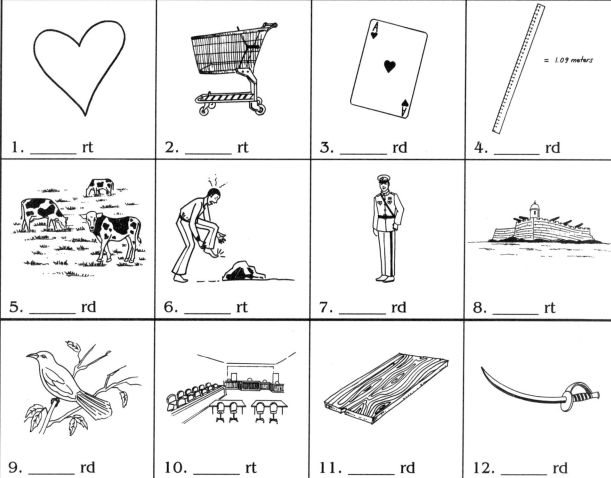

1. _____ rt

2. _____ rt

3. _____ rd

4. _____ rd

5. _____ rd

6. _____ rt

7. _____ rd

8. _____ rt

9. _____ rd

10. _____ rt

11. _____ rd

12. _____ rd

= 1.09 meters

Read

herd	herds	hurt	hurts
cord	cords	court	courts
card	cards	cart	carts

Listen • Write • Read

1. They painted their name on the _____.

2. You can buy a child's _____ in that store.

3. The tennis _____ are next to the school.

4. The _____ were singing all morning.

5. She drew three _____ on her paper.

Name it!   Final rl clusters

1. _____ rl

2. _____ rld

3. _____ rl

4. _____ l

5. _____ rl

6. _____ el

Read	**Add s**	**Add ed**
curl	curl ___	curl ___
pearl	pearl ___	
share	girl ___	
barrel	barrel ___	

Listen • Write • Read

1. She has beautiful blonde _____.

2. The _____ are full of water.

3. Mrs. Brown has four boys and two _____.

4. The _____ eat nuts and live in our tree.

5. Her husband bought her a necklace made of _____.

Sounds Easy!©2002 Alta Book Center Publishers, San Francisco, California
Permission granted to photocopy for one teacher's classroom use only.

Name it!   Final rf and rv clusters

1. _____ rf

2. _____ rf

3. _____ rf

4. _____ rve

5. _____ rve

6. _____ rve

Read	Add __s__	Add __ed__	Read	Add __ves__
curve	curve ___	curve ___	wharf	whar ___
carve	carve ___	carve ___	scarf	scar ___
serve	serve ___	serve ___		
surf	surf ___			

Listen • Write • Read

1. Some women wear _____ when it is windy.

2. The mountain road climbed and _____.

3. Let's go fishing on the _____.

4. The waitress _____ the dinner.

5. Father _____ the turkey on the holiday.

Review Vocabulary

1. _____	2. _____	3. _____	4. _____
5. _____	6. _____	7. = 1.09 meters _____	8. _____
9. _____	10. _____	11. _____	12. _____
13. _____	14. _____	15. _____	16. _____

Name it!

1. _____ rm

2. _____ rn

3. _____ rm

4. _____ rn

5. _____ rm

6. _____ rm

7. _____ rn

8. _____ rn

Read	Add _s_	Add _ed_
form	form ___	form ___
warm	warm ___	warm ___
storm	storm ___	storm ___
turn	turn ___	turn ___
burn	burn ___	burn ___

Listen • Write • Read

1. Herman _____ his _____ in the sun.

2. My jacket is _____.

3. There are many _____ in the garden.

4. Luisa made a sweater with yellow _____.

5. The old _____ was painted red.

6. Mother _____ the bread in the oven.

Name it!

1. _____ rge

2. _____ rch

3. _____ rge

4. _____ rch

5. _____ rch

6. _____ rch

7. _____ rch

8. _____ rch

Read	Add _d_
enlarge	enlarge ___
charge	charge ___

Read	Add _ed_
perch	perch ___
march	march ___
search	search ___

Listen • Write • Read

1. The children _____ to the music.

2. The bird _____ in the apple tree.

3. Did you _____ for your keys?

4. Yes, I _____ everywhere for them.

5. Can you _____ this on your VISA?

6. The month after February is _____.

7. A photograph that is made bigger is

_____.

8. A _____ number of people came

to her party.

Name it!   Final rb and rp clusters

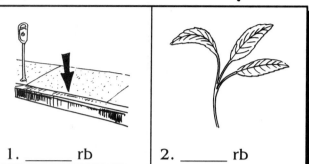

1. _____ rb | 2. _____ rb

JUMP
DANCE
WORK
CLEAN
DRIVE

3. _____ rbs | 4. _____ rb | 5. _____ rb | 6. _____ p

Read	Add _s_	Add _ed_
curb	curb ___	curb ___
chirp	chirp ___	chirp ___
herb	herb ___	
verb	verb ___	
tarp	tarp ___	

Listen • Write • Read

1. Lisa cooked _____ in the soup.

2. We learned ten new English _____ today.

3. Do you like _____ music?

4. The birds _____ all morning in the sun.

5. He parked the motorcycle next to the _____.

6. Be careful! That knife is _____!

Name it!   **Final rs clusters**

	my little cat is very fat he always sat upon my hat.	
1. _____ rse	2. _____ rse	3. _____ rse

| 4. _____ rse | 5. _____ rst | 6. _____ rst | 7. _____ rst |

Read	**Add _d_**	**Read**	**Add _s_**
nurse	nurse ___	thirst	thirst ___
force	force ___	burst	burst ___
verse	verse ___	first	first ___

Listen • Write • Read

1. The _____ was very kind to her patient.

2. The balloon _____ when the cat played with it.

3. Is this your mother's _____?

4. Is this the _____ time you've visited New York City?

5. Shelly writes beautiful English _____.

6. Gene _____ the sick dog for four days.

Name it!

1. _____ rk

2. _____ rk

3. _____ rk

4. _____ rk

Read	**Add s**	**Add ed**
bark	bark ___	bark ___
park	park ___	park ___
mark	mark ___	mark ___
work	work ___	work ___

Listen • Write • Read

1. That dog _____ all night!

2. Does it _____ every night?

3. Let's go to the _____.

4. James _____ seven nights a week last month.

5. This month he _____ only five nights.

6. The teacher _____ all the papers "correct."

7. The carpenter _____ his truck in the front yard.

Review Vocabulary

1. _____	2. _____	3. _____	4. _____
5. _____	6. _____	7. _____	8. _____
9. _____	10. _____	11. _____	12. _____
13. _____	14. _____	15. _____	16. _____

Review Vocabulary

1. _____

2. _____

3. _____

4. _____

5. _____

6. _____

7. _____

8. _____

9. _____

10. _____

11. _____

12. _____

13. _____

14. _____

15. _____

16. _____

Review Vocabulary

1. _____	2. _____	3. _____	4. _____
5. _____	6. _____	7. _____	8. _____
9. _____	10. _____	11. _____	12. _____
13. _____	14. _____	15. _____	16. _____

Review Vocabulary

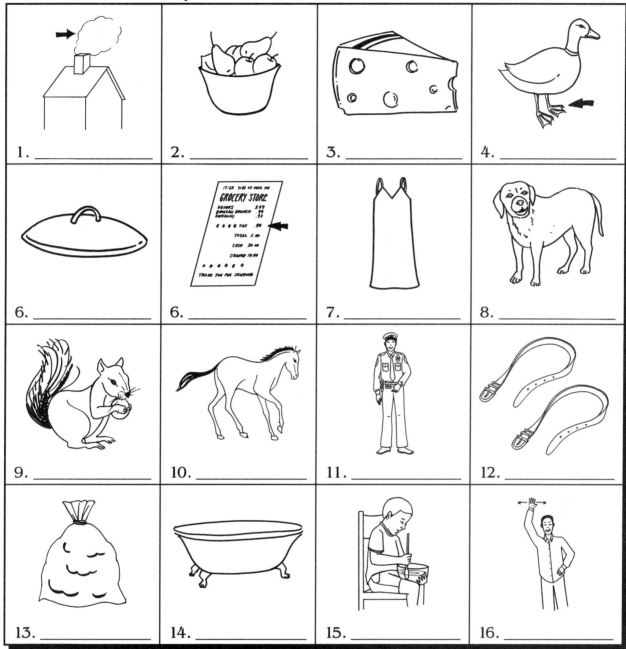

1. _____

2. _____

3. _____

4. _____

6. _____

6. _____

7. _____

8. _____

9. _____

10. _____

11. _____

12. _____

13. _____

14. _____

15. _____

16. _____

Name it!

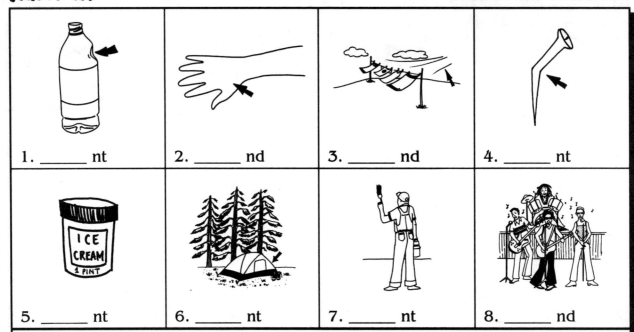

1. _____ nt	2. _____ nd	3. _____ nd	4. _____ nt
5. _____ nt	6. _____ nt	7. _____ nt	8. _____ nd

Read	Add _s_	Read	Add _s_
pant	pant ___	band	band ___
dent	dent ___	hand	hand ___
paint	paint ___	wind	wind ___
pint	pint ___	bend	bend ___
bent	bent ___	land	land ___

Listen • Write • Read

1. I like your new _____.

2. Did you go to see that rock and roll _____?

3. He _____ pictures of trees and flowers.

4. Did you wash your _____, Johnnie?

5. Four _____ equal one quart.

6. United Airlines flight number 461 _____ at 10 o'clock.

7. Can you _____ over and touch your toes?

Name it!

Final n clusters

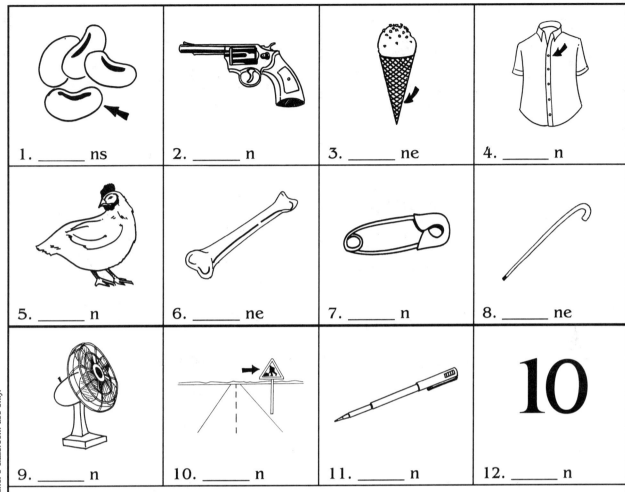

1. _____ ns

2. _____ n

3. _____ ne

4. _____ n

5. _____ n

6. _____ ne

7. _____ n

8. _____ ne

9. _____ n

10. _____ n

11. _____ n

12. _____ n

Read	**Add _s_**	**Add _ed_**
button	button ___	button ___
pin	pin ___	
fan	fan ___	

Listen • Write • Read

1. Lili _____ her sweater when she went outside.

2. The teacher _____ the name tags on the students.

3. Do you eat brown _____ for dinner sometimes?

4. We need _____ in the classroom in July. It's so hot!

Name it!

Final m clusters

1. _____ m	2. _____ me	3. _____ mb	4. _____ me
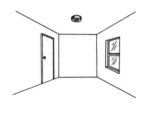			
5. _____ m	6. _____ mb	7. _____ mb	8. _____ me

Read	**Add s**	**Add ed**
comb	comb ___	comb ___
climb	climb ___	climb ___
lamb	lamb ___	
dime	dime ___	
home	home ___	
room	room ___	

Listen • Write • Read

1. She _____ her daughter's hair.

2. My little cat has _____ that tree many times.

3. How many _____ do you have in your house?

4. He gave her eight _____ in change.

5. The family's _____ are in Mexico.

6. Did you see the _____ on the farm?

Name it!   Final mp clusters

1. _____ mp

2. _____ mp

3. _____ mp

4. _____ mp

5. _____ mp

Read	**Add _s_**	**Add _ed_**
pump	pump ___	pump ___
camp	camp ___	camp ___
jump	jump ___	jump ___
stamp	stamp ___	stamp ___

Listen • Write • Read

1. Did you put _____ on the letter?

2. Yes, I _____ it.

3. The children _____ on the bed.

4. Sally and Ron _____ in the mountains together.

5. Ron _____ alone usually.

6. Luis is a mechanic. He _____ gasoline.

Name it!

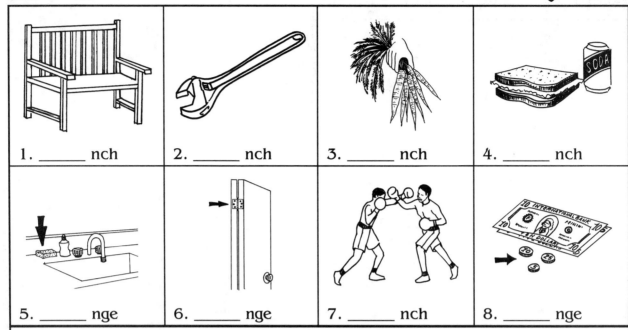

1. _____ nch

2. _____ nch

3. _____ nch

4. _____ nch

5. _____ nge

6. _____ nge

7. _____ nch

8. _____ nge

Read	Add **ed**	Read	Add **d**
bunch	bunch ___	change	change ___
lunch	lunch ___	hinge	hinge ___
		sponge	sponge ___

Listen • Write • Read

1. The two girls sat on the park _____.

2. Millie likes to take a bath with a _____.

3. The _____ on the closet door is broken.

5. Did you eat _____ yesterday?

5. Father had to _____ the tire on the car.

6. Then he _____ his shirt because it was dirty!

Name it!   Final ng and nk clusters

1. _____ ng

2. _____ nk

3. _____ nk

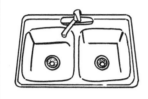

4. _____ nk

5. _____ ng

6. _____ ng

Read	**Add _s_**
ring	ring ___
ink	ink ___
sing	sing ___
swing	swing ___

Listen • Write • Read

1. He gave his wife two diamond _____!

2. There is so much _____ in our garage.

3. The plumber put new _____ in our house.

4. He _____ in the opera.

5. The children played in the park on the _____.

Review Vocabulary

1. _____	2. _____	**10** **10** 3. _____	4. _____
5. _____	6. _____	7. _____	8. _____
ICE CREAM 1 PINT 9. _____	10. _____	11. _____	12. _____
13. _____	14. _____	African Violet 29¢ 15. _____	16. _____

Review Vocabulary

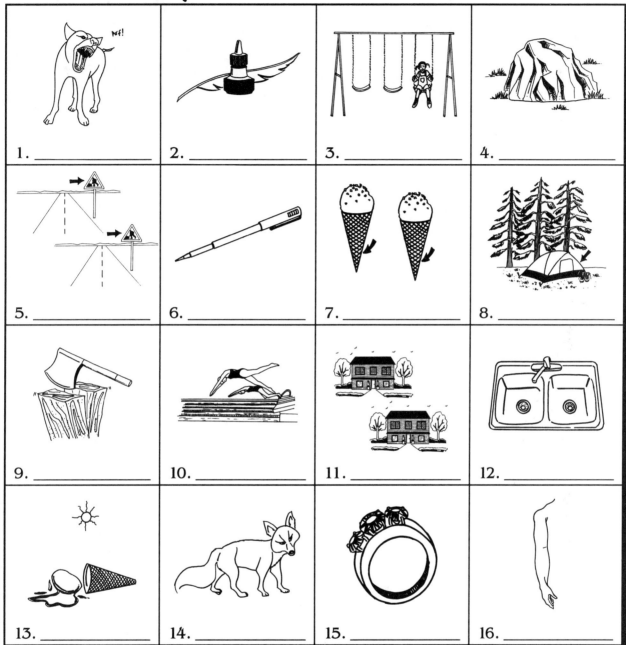

1. _____

2. _____

3. _____

4. _____

5. _____

6. _____

7. _____

8. _____

9. _____

10. _____

11. _____

12. _____

13. _____

14. _____

15. _____

16. _____

Review Vocabulary

1. _____

2. _____

3. _____

4. _____

5. _____

6. _____

7. _____

8. _____

9. _____

10. _____

11. _____

12. _____

13. _____

14. _____

15. _____

16. _____

Name it!

| 1. _____ sk | 2. _____ sc | 3. _____ sk | 4. _____ sk |

Read	**Add _s_**	**Add _ed_**
ask	ask ___	ask ___
mask	mask ___	mask ___
desk	desk ___	
disc	disc ___	
tusk	tusk ___	

Listen • Write • Read

1. Did you _____ a question?

2. Yes, I _____, "What time is it?"

3. Everyone will wear _____ to the party.

4. An elephant has _____, not teeth.

5. Is this your _____?

6. A _____ man robbed the bank.

7. I want to buy a new compact _____ player.

Name it!

		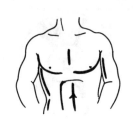	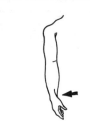
1. _____ ste	2. _____ st	3. _____ st	4. _____ st
	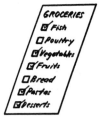		
5. _____ ste	6. _____ st	7. _____ st	8. _____ st

Read	**Add _s_**
paste	paste ___
list	list ___
nest	nest ___
wrist	wrist ___
vest	vest ___

Listen • Write • Read

1. Lucy likes to _____ all the things she needs to buy.

2. She's wearing a gold bracelet on her _____.

3. The birds build small _____ in our trees.

4. Mom cooked a _____ for Thanksgiving.

5. A _____ is good to wear on a cold day.

6. I keep my papers in a locked _____.

7. _____ is a kind of glue to stick paper.

8. Sherry threw the letter in the _____ basket.

Name it!   **Final z and s clusters**

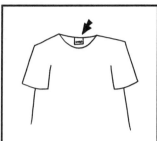

1. _____ ze

2. _____ se

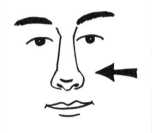

3. _____ se

4. _____ se

5. _____ zz

6. _____ se

Read	Add _s_	Add _d_
raise	raise ___	raise ___
close	close ___	close ___
size	size ___	
nose	nose ___	
rose	rose ___	

Listen • Write • Read

1. The students _____ their hands before speaking.

2. The bee _____ around the flower in my garden.

3. She buys both _____ medium and large.

4. Who _____ the door?

5. Martin always _____ the windows before leaving.

6. Was she picking the _____ this morning?

7. Can he fix the _____ on the washing machine?

Review Vocabulary

1. _____	2. _____	3. _____	4. _____
5. _____	6. _____	7. _____	8. _____
9. _____	10. _____	11. _____	12. _____
13. _____	14. _____	15. _____	16. _____

Name it!   Final th clusters

1. _____ th

2. _____ th

3. _____ th

4. _____ th

5. _____ th

6. _____ th

Read

moth

bath

path

mouth

Add _s_

moth ____

bath ____

path ____

mouth ____

Listen • Write • Read

1. The _____ cross when they come to the river.

2. She takes two _____ a day.

3. The _____ like to fly near the light.

4. Seven children! So many _____ to feed!

5. Do you live in the north or the _____ part of the country?

Reference Charts

(Photocopiable)

Alphabet Chart

A _____ B _____ C _____

a _____ b _____ c _____

D _____ E _____ F _____

d _____ e _____ f _____

G _____ H _____ I _____

g _____ h _____ i _____

J _____ K _____ L _____

j _____ k _____ l _____

M _____ N _____ O _____

m _____ n _____ o _____

P _____ Q _____ R _____

p _____ q _____ r _____

S _____ T _____ U _____

s _____ t _____ u _____

V _____ W _____ X _____

v _____ w _____ x _____

Y _____ Z _____

y _____ z _____

Consonants Chart

b	c	d	f	B	C	D	F
g	l	m	p	G	L	M	P
t	h	s	k	T	H	S	K
r	j	n	v	R	J	N	V
q	w	x	z	Q	W	X	Z
			sh	SH			
			ch	CH			
			ph	PH			
			th	TH			

Vowels Chart

a _____   A _____

i _____   I _____

e _____   E _____

o _____   O _____

u _____   U _____

a	a c<u>a</u>n	a c<u>a</u>k<u>e</u>	a r<u>ai</u>n	a d<u>ay</u>	
i	i g<u>i</u>ft	i f<u>i</u>r<u>e</u>	i t<u>ie</u>	i n<u>igh</u>t	
e	e b<u>e</u>ll	e tr<u>ee</u>	e r<u>ea</u>d		
o	o cl<u>o</u>ck	o b<u>oa</u>t	o r<u>o</u>s<u>e</u>	o thr<u>ow</u>	o t<u>oe</u>
u	u tr<u>u</u>ck	u t<u>u</u>b<u>e</u>	u r<u>u</u>l<u>e</u>	u fr<u>ui</u>t	

Sounds Easy!©2002 Alta Book Center Publishers, San Francisco, California
Permission granted to photocopy for one teacher's classroom use only.

Initial Clusters Chart

blue	brown		play	price
clean	cream		glad	green
flag	fruit		tree	drink
this	three		stop	strong
she	shrimp		skirt	scratch
	sport	splash	spring	
	small	snow	sleep	

Sounds Easy!©2002 Alta Book Center Publishers, San Francisco, California
Permission granted to photocopy for one teacher's classroom use only.

Final Clusters Chart

robs	robbed		maps	mapped	
cats	beds		watch	watched	
cage	caged		fish	fished	
bags	bagged		smokes	smoked	
tax	taxed		moves	moved	leaves
cold	colds		salt	salts	
fires	fired		calls	called	
cards	hurts		curls	curled	
warms	warmed		turns	turned	
march	marched		carves	carved	
curbs	chirped		parks	parked	
nurse	first	thirsts			
paint	paints		land	lands	
pins	pinned		comb	combs	combed
pump	pumps	pumped	lunch	lunched	
bank	banks	banked	ask	asks	asked
waste	wastes	closed			
breathes	breathed				